The
INNOVATION
GENERATION

The Gen Y Way & How New Thinking
Can Reclaim the American Dream

by Jenny Floren

Founder of Experience.com—bridging the gap
between education and business for 15 years.

THE INNOVATION GENERATION
The Gen Y Way & How New Thinking
Can Reclaim the American Dream

ISBN 978-0-9671565-1-4 (paperback)
ISBN 978-1-935547-16-7 (hardcover)

Written by Jenny Floren
Editing by Michael Dowding, Wordscape Communications, Inc.
Copyediting by Cindy Beatty, Proof Positive Papers
Cover design by Katrina Monsees, Jayashree Patel, and Val Sherer
Interior design and layout by Val Sherer, Personalized Publishing Services
Photography by Amy Wong

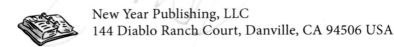

New Year Publishing, LLC
144 Diablo Ranch Court, Danville, CA 94506 USA

To all the innovators who never let what *is*
stand in the way of what's *possible*.

Foreword

Innovation has always been America's most important weapon for success. We have innovated our way to new sources of revenue and growth; we have innovated our way to cure diseases; and we have innovated our way to create entirely new markets that have increased prosperity around the world. The time has come for America to re-start its engine of innovation—our future depends on it. But exactly how to do that remains elusive, despite our investment of trillions of dollars in search of solutions. However, there is an approach we haven't yet considered—and it may hold the answer for how to kick-start American innovation and recovery. The solutions we need may come from an unexpected source, a resource that sits right before our eyes, waiting for us to recognize its potential …

Something very profound has been happening over the past two decades. A new generation, Generation Y, was born between 1978-2000, and has come of age using the Internet, watching live, 24/7 news, expecting instant communications and emerging as the world's first generation of "digital natives." For the first time in history, these children have adopted the newest technologies before the adults, and they have become the experts of the wired frontier. Today's global economy brings new challenges and new rules, it is a new world—and Gen Y speaks the native tongue fluently. Their unique perspective and new thinking—the *Gen Y Way*—is a powerful asset, if we're willing to recognize and leverage its potential.

Traditionally, the entry-level workforce has been seen as a source of overhead—with the assumption that we must incur extensive costs *before* they can contribute to our success. However, today it's different—for the first time in history, the emerging talent market also brings with it a powerful new expertise, a new level of tech-savvy, and a new socially-conscious, global perspective that has been shaped by the world in which they have grown up. They are fluent in the language of this new world, and the new thinking of the *Gen Y Way* is particularly well suited for success in the high-stakes, fast-moving global economy. While the Internet may have seemed like a fad just 10 years ago, it is now considered central to any business growth strategy—and the Internet is the natural habitat of Gen Y. Similarly, one-to-one marketing, search engine optimization, global competition, social networking, environmentally-friendly production, corporate citizenship—these are all key success factors that are relatively new to most of us, but not to Gen Y. These concepts have been part of their world since day one, and they have developed knowledge, perspective, attitudes and aptitudes that can make a significant contribution to innovate and grow. Their input can add tremendous value right now—in fact, their input may be exactly what we need to get America back on track.

Too often, investment in up-and-coming talent is considered an optional "nice-to-have" that is prioritized below other investments; it's seen as a tactical requirement to fill open jobs, or as altruism that helps students, or as a long-term investment for social or economic benefit that will pay off someday in the distant future. When corporations invest resources, it's usually through their resource-constrained corporate foundations or human resources departments, not through mainline business management. In business, investing in entry-level talent is seen as a tactical HR task, not as a strategic issue that has a direct impact on revenue, profitability, and the organization's ability to successfully compete in the new global economy.

This is old thinking. And this old thinking no longer works.

There is more than enough evidence that investing to prepare young talent is the right thing to do for long-term social benefit—the correlation between an educated population and economic prosperity has been proven in the U.S. and in many countries around the world.

But there is another reason that investing in entry-level talent makes sense—and that is to leverage the unique new thinking of the *Gen Y Way* to <u>accelerate</u> innovation… to create growth, profitability, and competitive advantage today. As examples throughout this book demonstrate, businesses should invest *for their own benefit*—not just out of goodwill for students or long-term social impact. Businesses have an opportunity to capitalize on the unique strengths of the emerging "digital natives" to deliver powerful business results—if we stop viewing them as unprepared overhead, and begin to appreciate and incorporate their contributions *now*.

Today America faces many challenges, and we all have many questions about how to get our country back on a path toward a better future—the Innovation Generation may have the answers.

Acknowledgements

Millions of people have contributed to the creation of this book. *Literally.*

Every one of the five million college graduates in the Experience network serves as an inspiration to me and to our team—and to the next generation of talent, I give my heartfelt thanks. Thank you for using your new thinking to re-start America's engine of innovation. I know you can do it ....

Special thanks to my family, friends, and the entire Experience team—including our peeps, clients, partners, investors, advisors, students, graduates, employers, and fans. Thank you all for making this adventure possible!

And to all of you who helped me write, review, edit, proofread and polish this book—I don't know where to begin to thank you. Janet Sun, you are a life saver. Michael Dowding, you are a saint. Robbie, you are my hero.

Contents

CHAPTER 1

What Have We Done?

"Today I say to you that the challenges we face are real. They are serious and they are many."

President Barack Obama, 2009

I n so many ways, 2009 marked an epic crossroads for America. Inflection points are everywhere. In politics, economics, foreign policy, religion, technology, education, healthcare, the environment—and even our media and culture—we face choices and challenges that are sobering in their complexity and unsettling in their resistance to easy (or even plausible) solutions.

Despite what many view as a fresh start in our new president, beneath our veneer of hope and optimism lies a long list of questions about how we're going to get America back on track. For many of us, as we survey the landscape of challenges, we come to an ominous realization: we are running out of time.

It is becoming increasingly obvious that the game has somehow changed—the stakes are higher, the rules seem different, and our go-to solutions that have helped us out of crises in the past no longer seem able to close the floodgates. As our institutions, government, and citizens attempt to pull us out of what seems like a downward spiral, it feels to many like we're struggling in quicksand—every move seems to make matters worse, not better. According to Craig Barrett, chairman of Intel, "We are watching the decline and fall of the U.S. as an economic power—not hypothetically, but as we speak."[1] We need answers to some very serious questions—and the clock is ticking.

How much more can our country afford?

Our macroeconomic climate is perhaps as daunting as any we've encountered in the past 80 years. Financial experts toss around eye-popping bailout figures that are impossible for most of us to truly comprehend. The hangover of spending trillions of dollars— with an outcome that is far from predictable or certain—will be felt for generations. On the current trajectory, *interest payments* on our debt will soon become the single largest expenditure of our federal budget—larger than Social Security, Medicare and Medicaid, or even national defense.[2] While the benefits of the unprecedented government spending in 2009/2010 are far from certain, it's crystal clear that the expenditures related to the financial sector, the auto and manufacturing sectors, and healthcare reform will have repercussions that all citizens will need to wrestle with, today and well into our future. Even the U.S. government needs to balance its budget eventually. How will we find a way to do this?

Historically we have relied on the American consumer to fund our budgets. Since 1950, the consumer's share of GDP spending (including housing) has ranged from 66-76 percent. Between income taxes and consumer spending, our citizens have served as a primary source of capital, fueling our economic engine of growth. This time it's different; the game has changed and the old rules no longer apply. Unemployment persists, consumer debts remain unpaid, healthcare costs continue to climb, and the increasing burden on American taxpayers seems to have no end in sight. As U.S. Economics Editor Greg Ip reports in *The Economist*, consumer debt increased from an average of 80 percent of disposable income in the late 1980s to more than 125 percent of income in 2007. Furthermore, American household wealth has declined by $12 trillion, or 18 percent, since 2007; and as consumers feel that pinch, they are less inclined to spend.[3] As unemployment endures, we face an increased risk that an entire generation of young people may suffer lifelong consequences as a 'lost generation,' similar to what Japan experienced following its decade-long economic slump in the 1990s that pushed an entire generation of young talent out of the labor market—with little to no chance of *ever* catching up during their lifetimes.[4]

Furthermore, as Baby Boomers reach retirement age, the unyielding laws of demography point to one of our country's most important inflection points of all: significantly more people are leaving the workforce (and our tax base) than are entering. How will we achieve financial stability when our country has more elderly citizens to care for and fewer workers contributing to our economy?

The burden will clearly fall to our children and, despite our willingness to pass along these enormous problems, we seem unwilling to take the necessary steps to prepare our children to handle them successfully. The vast web of complexity that we call our "education system" has proven largely incapable of supporting our true goal: to prepare the next generation of Americans for a successful future. From inconsistent curriculum standards to inaccessible financial aid to questionable teacher compensation policies, we have created one of our country's most widespread and intractable problems. Many in Washington point fingers at those in the state government (because states control the majority of funding and control over education), many in the state government point fingers at the teachers unions (primarily because the unions control the power—they are the de facto governing body of influence over the 14,000 distinct and separate school districts that set the rules for how our nation's children will be prepared for the future), and, in the name of protecting teachers, the unions ferociously resist reform (because they fear they have the most to lose from change). Meanwhile, the ramifications of this dysfunctional system are clear: American children are falling behind those in other countries, more Americans are dropping out of school, employers are less satisfied with the labor market available to grow our economy, and fewer Americans have a fair chance to succeed in the increasingly competitive global labor market. This raises the most important question of all:

How will America *survive* if our people aren't prepared to succeed?

These are not easy questions. These are not small problems. There are no 'silver bullet' solutions ... but there *is* a way out of this mess. And there are signs of hope that the citizens of our country have finally had enough and are willing to do what it takes to change our course and aim toward a better future.

After what feels like decades of simply leaving the problems to the next generation, there's a sense today that punting is no longer an option; the challenges are finally too great to ignore. For too long, we have been under-investing in longer-term, sustainable, transformational solutions, favoring instead a patchwork of short-term fixes aimed at incremental improvement. We have tolerated the status quo and stood by while the distance between the 'haves' and 'have-nots' has grown farther and farther apart. We have spent our time and money (and then took on debt so we could spend even more time and money) on attempts to fund band-aid solutions that address the symptoms, but not the root cause. We can't afford to play that game anymore. That game has ended. Those days are over. The bill, as they say, has come due.

And you know what? *That's the good news.*

This wake-up call is long overdue. Finally, it is loud enough for all of us to hear it. With the future of our country and the survival of the American Dream hanging in the balance, we all sense the urgent need to find solutions. We need a new path forward, and we need it *now*—we don't have any more time to waste.

CHAPTER 2

Innovation Is Our (Only) Way Out

"It is not the strongest of the species, nor the most intelligent, that survives. It is the one that is most adaptable to change."

Charles Darwin

When trying to solve complex problems with many facets and interrelated components, it's helpful to break down the challenge to its most essential pieces and determine what must be solved first. Janet Kraus, the entrepreneurial co-founder of Circles and Spire.com, reminded me of this helpful analogy:

"Let's say your challenge is to put a big rock, a bunch of small pebbles, and a handful of sand into a single glass jar. How do you make them all fit? The trick is to place them inside the jar in the right order. By putting the big rock in first, followed by the pebbles, and then the sand, you can get them all into the jar. If you don't put the big rock in first, you won't be able to fit it in after the pebbles and the sand. Getting the big rock in place *first* is the only way to make it work."

As we contemplate how to get America back on track, perhaps the most vital question we must answer is: which problem is the 'big rock' that must be solved *first*?

With the list of issues facing our country, this is no small task. It's hard to argue that fixing K-12 education is more important than addressing the healthcare system, or that healthcare reform is more important than global warming or energy independence, or that energy is more important than avoiding the collapse of the financial system. They are all important, they are all urgent, and they are all high-impact issues that have ramifications for every citizen and the success of our country.

The problem is that *not one* of these issues is the 'big rock.' Although these are the challenges that seem to get the most headlines, the most attention in Washington, and the most coverage on CNN, none of these represent the biggest, most fundamental issue facing our nation. They are merely *symptoms* of our problem, the evidence of our more fundamental breakdown. As significant as these challenges are, they are the pebbles that can only be addressed after the big rock is put in place first.

So what's the 'big rock'?

Houston (and Denver, and New York, and San Francisco, and...)—
We've Got a Problem.

In February 2008, two global companies were competing for one of the largest defense contracts ever awarded by the United States government, a nearly $40 billion contract for the manufacture of military aerial refueling tankers. After years of negotiations, the U.S. Air Force delivered a stunning blow to U.S.-based Boeing by awarding the contract to Airbus, a French division of the European Aeronautic Defense & Space Company that had partnered with Northrop Grumman to submit its bid. The decision by our Air Force to award a national security contract to a non-U.S. company caused heated outrage and protest, and the contract still remains in a holding pattern to this day.[5]

While multi-billion-dollar contracts are inherently complex propositions in which a wide variety of criteria receive lengthy consideration, at least one underlying reason for the award to Airbus lay in our government's skepticism that Boeing could recruit the necessary number of qualified, skilled professionals to work on the multi-year project. The frank and shocking implication: the United States might not have enough talent to get the job done.

What?

To anyone concerned about the future of America, the very possibility of a talent crisis should sound a code-red alarm. The

2009 financial crisis will seem like a garden party compared to the consequences of a talent crisis—and no amount of treasury-printed money can fix it. Changing the tide of a talent crisis requires investments socially, culturally, and systematically throughout all corners of our nation—and those take *time*. To avoid a talent crisis today, we should have started our investments 20-30 years ago (just as China and India did).

But late is better than never, and if our country is to have any hope of retaining our global leadership, we must improve. We will not succeed if our people are not prepared for success. *And the way we're preparing our people is not working.* When one of our country's pioneering companies struggles to win contracts from our own government, we should all take it as a serious wake-up call. If we aren't able to develop the talent within our people to sustain a competitive labor market, we will lose our ability to compete in the global economy—and we may never get it back.

American Innovation

From the cotton gin, railroads, and telephones to automobiles, cameras, vaccinations, space exploration, computers, mass media, telecommunications, and the Internet, America has been the breeding ground and proving ground for the world's biggest breakthroughs. It is no accident that throughout our innovative history, America has also been the nation with the most educated population, and the nation with the most direct access to the thought leaders who could be found within the educational institutions, companies, and organizations at the forefront of knowledge, R&D, and innovation.

Success, as they say, happens when preparation meets opportunity. The virtuous circle works like this: an educated and prepared talent pool gives employers reason to hire them, which gives people hands-on work experience and the exposure to problems that must be solved. And when those problems are seen through the lens of 'fresh eyes' that bring new perspectives, it leads to new ideas and new inventions, which in turn fuel the launch of new markets and new businesses, which create new jobs. New jobs generate more income and opportunities for more people, who can then afford more education and opportunity for their children, who can then contribute as participants in the workforce ... and the cycle begins anew.

When the Internet and the information age swept the world with a wave of game-changing innovation, America led the way. From the underlying infrastructure and technology to software applications and creative new business models, the companies leading the world in innovation throughout that era were primarily American: Microsoft, Google, Cisco, Amazon, eBay, Yahoo!, Salesforce.com, Akamai ... and the list goes on. As a result, enormous numbers of jobs, investment funding, training opportunities, and income were generated—starting in America, and subsequently extending around the world. America led the way in innovation and, as a result, also led the way in the gains and benefits derived as a result of the innovation.

Today, we are losing ground. We are losing our leadership position. In the race toward the next frontier of world-changing innovation, America is behind—and falling further back. Many believe that the innovations and opportunities to be found in the new energy sector (specifically stemming from clean technologies and renewable energy) will dwarf the enormous growth delivered by the personal computer and Internet eras combined. Just imagine what a market of that scope could generate in terms of follow-on benefits in the form of companies, jobs, earnings, and opportunities created as a result of the innovation. Now consider this: where do you think those jobs, earnings, and opportunities will take place? If history is any indication, the jobs and prosperity follow the innovation—and the innovation is not happening in America. Today, only four of the top 30 companies leading the way in solar, wind, and battery development are in the United States. *Four.* Hosting fewer than 15 percent of the leading innovators hardly qualifies as a leadership position in what many expect will be the next major frontier of global economic growth.

As John Doerr, one of the world's leading venture capitalists, wrote in an article co-written with General Electric CEO Jeff Immelt, "We are clearly not in the lead today. That position is held by China, which understands the importance of controlling its energy future. China's commitment to developing clean energy technologies and markets is breathtaking. Consider: Chinese cars are more than one-third more fuel-efficient than U.S. cars. China is investing 10 times as much on clean power, as a percentage of gross domestic product, as the United States is. China is on track to create 150,000 jobs through the deployment of 120 gigawatts of wind power by 2020—an amount equivalent to today's global total and nearly five times America's. As a result, China is already curbing its carbon emissions substantially. This year alone, it will abate almost 350 million tons of carbon dioxide, as compared with business as usual. That's as much as is emitted by Argentina."[6]

A recent study by the International Technology & Innovation Foundation suggested that the U.S. ranks sixth among 40 countries evaluated in terms of their innovation.[7] That finding is ample cause for alarm, given that the U.S. has led the modern world in essentially every other wave of significant innovation.

But that was not the most shocking conclusion of the study. The ITIF study also rated the U.S. *dead last* for our rate of change to prepare for the next wave of innovation. In more than 16 key metrics spanning human capital development, entrepreneurship, innovation, infrastructure, and economic policy, the United States showed the slowest rate of improvement over the last decade.[8] That means *every* other country on the list is accelerating its pace of innovation *faster* than the U.S. The writing is on the wall, and it's in BIG, BOLD LETTERS.

The BIG Rock

I contend that the most important problem our country must address *first* is not education, healthcare, energy, immigration, or even ending the wars. The single most important thing we need to do as a nation—the 'big rock' that our country needs to solve before a solution to any of our other problems will be possible—is to re-start our engine of innovation. This is not just about the education system; although having a population with a basic foundation of competency is certainly a piece of the solution, the solutions required extend far outside the four walls of the classroom. The focus of our efforts should be marshalling every ounce of our time, creativity, energy, and resources *to stimulate innovation.*

The Case for Innovation

The term 'innovation' can seem so vague and amorphous that it's sometimes difficult to consider how to get our arms around it. To break it down into more tangible and actionable terms, let's walk step-by-step through some very simple (and perhaps overly simplified) logic behind the direct, simple, and fundamental connections that tie innovation to our ultimate goal of broad and lasting prosperity.

To begin, let's consider what it takes to create prosperity. At the most basic level, we might say that prosperity includes having base needs accounted for—health, safety, food, shelter—and the opportunity to secure a good life for our children. [It's not my intention to get philosophical about the meaning of life *per se*, but simply to ground the conversation in a concrete, fundamental goal that we can all personally relate to and agree upon: no matter how diverse our personal experiences may be, we all share a common humanity, and the basic desire to create a better world for the future has been shared by religions, nations, ethnicities, races, and humans around the globe and throughout the course of time.]

As Amar Bhide, a visiting professor at Harvard's Kennedy School of Government explains, "The measure of a good economy lies in the satisfaction it provides to the many, not a few...and these satisfactions go beyond the material or pecuniary rewards earned: they include, for instance, the exhilaration of overcoming challenges. Indeed they go hand in hand: a good economy cannot provide widespread prosperity without harnessing the creativity and enterprise of the many. All must have the opportunity to innovate, to try out new things: not just scientists and engineers but also graphic artists, shop floor workers, salespersons and advertising agencies; not just the developers of new products but their venturesome consumers. The exceptional performance of a few high-tech businesses, as the Silicon Valley and Israeli examples show, is just not enough."[9]

So how does innovation relate to shared and sustained prosperity? It's not only a direct, straight-line connection—in my opinion, it's the *only* way to get there.

No. 1: Jobs are a key ingredient of prosperity—for more than one reason.

Access to jobs is a key ingredient in the recipe for prosperity. One reason jobs are so important is obvious: they are a source of income, and income is necessary to cover the costs of basic needs and wants. But that's not the only reason jobs matter so much. Jobs are not simply economic units that underlie the transfer of currency in an economy. They are also fundamental to social fabric. Jobs help give people a sense of purpose and a way to contribute—whether to a company, a church, a government, a tribe, or a household. When it comes to breaking the cycle of poverty, extensive research has demonstrated that access to jobs not only provides people with important income, but also builds self-confidence, reduces alcohol and drug abuse, keeps families together, and even improves parental engagement in their children's education. Because of their impact on children and families, jobs play an important role in creating long-term cycles of prosperity that lead to a better future.

Keeping people in jobs really matters. In his compelling review of the American job market, *The Atlantic* Deputy Managing Editor Don Peck warned, "If it persists much longer, this era of high joblessness will likely change the course and character of a generation of young adults—and quite possibly those of the children behind them as well … It may already by plunging many inner cities into a kind of despair and dysfunction not seen for decades. Ultimately, it is likely to warp our politics, our culture, and the character of our society for years."[10]

When it comes to creating broad and lasting prosperity, as *The New York Times* columnist Nicholas Kristof puts so clearly, "Research shows what works: education and jobs. [That's what's needed to] break the self-destructive cycle of poverty: resignation, self-doubt, alcohol and drug abuse, disintegrating families, lack of engagement in children's education," and prevent the cycle from repeating.[11]

In this way, jobs are not only an outcome of prosperity, they are also a *cause* of prosperity.

No. 2: Innovation is the (only) way jobs get created—and the absence of innovation is the (almost only) reason jobs go away.

When politicians discuss jobs, it often sounds like jobs are things that are simply created on demand when the leaders of a big company hold a meeting in a plush conference room and make a decision to "just do it." Although it's possible to create jobs that way (such as when the government decided to hire thousands of people to manage census data collection), that's not really how the job-creation process works.

At the most basic, fundamental level, jobs exist to solve problems. When there is a problem that must be solved, a 'job' is created. Not all jobs are done by humans; technology can do jobs that solve certain problems, too—and can replace productive people. However, even when that happens and some jobs are lost to technological replacements, new jobs for people are also created: the acts of creating, managing, selling, delivering, maintaining, and using the technology are jobs for people. The key to this cycle is to understand that jobs follow problems that must be solved … and as problems evolve, the jobs to solve them evolve, too.

The problems we face today are becoming increasingly complex and therefore require more sophisticated solutions. There was a time when the problem of communicating a message from one person to another was solved by hopping on a horse and hand-delivering a letter. As the frontier expanded, the problem evolved—it became necessary to deliver messages over greater distances. And of course, as the problem evolved, the jobs required to solve the problem evolved, too. On April 3, 1860, Johnny Fry began the first leg of a multi-day, multi-horse, multi-rider journey from St. Joseph, Missouri, to Sacramento, California—and with the delivery of 49 letters and five telegrams, the innovation of the Pony Express came to life.[12]

Today, the problem of delivering communications has evolved, and there are dramatically different requirements for its solution: the message may need to be instantaneous, confidential and secure, rich in format and presentation (video and audio rather than hand-written), and archived for legal purposes. Addressing these new dimensions of the problem requires different jobs with different skills that stretch well beyond the ability to ride on horseback. Today, solving the evolved problem requires knowing how to create and launch satellites, write software, provide data infrastructures, and the like. As the problem has evolved, the jobs have evolved, too.

As demonstrated by the evolution of the communication industry, the world's problems are not only becoming more sophisticated in nature, but they are also expanding in geographic scope. This means that the jobs to solve next-generation problems not only require the ability to invent more advanced solutions, but they also require the ability to serve customers across the globe—not just across town.

With the rise of the middle class around the globe, Americans are no longer the only (or even the biggest) consumer market. The vast majority of customers are outside our country, so America's economic recovery depends on our ability to create new products and services that are desired—and can be purchased—by customers all around the world. Investing in high-value products and services that require sophisticated manufacturing or creative skills (such as medical devices or methods for capturing renewable energy) will be more valuable than manual-labor-intensive items or processes that can be more easily automated. It's important to note that high-value technology-enabled innovation is not limited to what is typically considered the 'technology sector'—even areas like the arts have evolved to require highly sophisticated innovation.

For example, although inexpensive digital technologies have supported a burgeoning film industry in countries like India and South Korea, Hollywood stands alone in its ability to marshal the technology, creativity, marketing, and industry expertise to create something like *Avatar* (which has earned more than $3 billion so far, the majority of which came from international sales).

In today's advanced world, much of the value of products and services is found in the smarts that go behind inventing them— and the highest wages follow. Apple's iPod is an example of an innovative product invented in America and assembled elsewhere (in China). Greg Linden and his colleagues at UC-Irvine estimate that although many jobs move off-shore to countries that provide lower-cost manufacturing, the majority of wages remain on shore. In fact, Americans, who contribute primarily in the areas of engineering, software, marketing, and distribution, make up $753 million, or 70 percent, of the $1.1 billion of total worldwide wages.[13] According to the researchers, "The iPod supports nearly twice as many jobs offshore as in the U.S., yet wages paid in the U.S. are over twice as much as those paid overseas." The innovators reap the rewards.

Barbara Kiviat of *Time* magazine did a deep dive entitled, "Jobs: where they are and how to find them."[14] Her evidence demonstrated that our discourse is too focused on creating jobs and not focused enough on the necessary conditions in which jobs can be created: when customers need what we're selling, because we're selling innovative new solutions that offer better, faster, or cheaper ways to solve problems. "In the long term, there is only one way to create enough jobs for the economy: innovation."

No. 3: People are the source of (all) innovation.

Despite the fascinating advances in artificial intelligence, robotics, and the like, people are the fundamental source of new ideas. Innovation, at its core, is simply the use of new ideas to solve problems in new and better ways. The key in the 21st-century global economy is that the problems are changing—they are much more sophisticated, they are global in scope, and they require more knowledge to solve them.

Through their efforts to develop an index to understand the economic factors underlying prosperity, economists Michael Porter, Christian Ketels, and Mercedes Delgado found that, "Advanced economies compete by producing innovative products and services at the global technology frontier using the most advanced methods."[15] In other words, to advance our economy and create new jobs, our people must identify new problems— and take steps to solve them in new ways. This means using our creativity to identify new markets, new customers, and new solutions that offer real value by solving problems better, faster, or cheaper than existing alternatives.

The capacity of people to think, create, and innovate has a direct and demonstrable link to measurable economic growth. Professor Eric Hanushek of Stanford University studied how the strength of "cognitive skills" within the workforce differentiated economic leaders from laggards among 50 countries from 1960 to 2000.[16] He found that, "A highly skilled workforce can raise the economic growth by about two-thirds of a percentage point every year" (and given that the worldwide average annual growth of GDP is 2-3 percent, that's a significant jump). "Higher levels of cognitive skill appear to play a major role in explaining international differences in economic growth."

Having the talent to support innovation isn't just about educating a few extraordinary rocket scientists. To succeed, the entire labor force must be prepared with the skills required to contribute. A study from the Massachusetts Institute of Technology found that, "The use of technology substitutes for workers who perform routine tasks, but complements workers who perform non-routine problem solving. Repetitive, predictable tasks are readily automated. Hence, computerization of the workplace has raised the demand for problem solving and communication tasks, such as responding to discrepancies, improving production processes, and coordinating and managing the activities of others."[17]

In other words, the routine jobs that can be automated *will* be automated ... and the primary (if not only) value-add from "people jobs" will come by contributing to *problem solving* and *idea generation.* Although we certainly need thought-leading inventors to lead innovation, their individual talent alone is not sufficient. Innovation also requires bench strength across the entire workforce to support an infrastructure that can bring new ideas to life. Innovation is a team sport—and it's a fast-moving game.

People and companies need to keep up to remain competitive. At Intel, products evolve so quickly that ninety percent of the products delivered on the final day of each year didn't exist on the first day of the same year.[18] Inventor and futurist Ray Kurzweil predicts that the rate of change will continue to become faster: "The twenty-first century will see almost a thousand times greater technological change than its predecessor."[19] According to the think-tank Partnership for 21st Century Skills, "An overwhelming 80% of American voters say the kind of skills students need to learn to be prepared for the jobs of this century are different than what they needed 20 years ago."[20] In fact, most of the jobs that this year's college graduates will be called on to perform over the course of their careers don't even exist yet.

Preparing people to keep up with the pace of innovation isn't just about teaching them the skills they need to solve today's problems—it's about preparing them to identify and solve *new* problems *again, and again, and again.* Innovation is the only way to achieve prosperity—therefore preparing and encouraging people to innovate is the most important component of any national agenda. As author Peter Senge emphasizes in his book, *The Fifth Discipline,* "The only sustainable competitive advantage is the ability to learn faster than your competition."[21]

Governments and employers around the world all understand that people are, by far, the most important asset contributing to success, growth, and sustained competitive advantage. According to the National Center on Education and the Economy, higher wages will go to the countries with top talent.[22] The NCEE reported that, "The best employers the world over will be looking for the most competent, most creative, and most innovative people on the face of the planet and will be willing to pay top dollar for their services. This will be true not just for the top professionals and managers, but up and down the length and breadth of the workforce. Those countries that produce the most important new products and services can capture a premium in the world markets that will enable them to pay a higher wages to *all* their citizens." As the world's problems are evolving, the jobs to solve them are evolving, too—and the countries with talent able to keep up are the ones that prosper.

What does it take to win the innovation game?

Innovation requires people—and the key to our success will be our ability to prepare and encourage our people to innovate. Although this may sound like a straightforward concept, it begs the question: how, exactly, will we do that? And, furthermore, how will we do that better than any other country we compete with in the global economy? If the world's problems are evolving faster and faster, and the jobs required to solve new problems are also evolving faster and faster, what do we need to do to keep up?

As Charles Darwin so famously pointed out, survival of the fittest depends on the ability to *adapt*. As the world's problems become more sophisticated, more complicated, more global in scope, and evolve at a faster pace—we must figure out a systematic way to *continuously* keep up.

If we are to re-start our engine of innovation, we need people to be prepared. The problems that need solving in the global 'knowledge economy' are sophisticated, and the only way to sustain competitive advantage is to lead the way with the best new ideas and innovation. As Thomas Friedman of *The New York Times* says so poignantly, "We might be able to stimulate our way back to stability, but we can only invent our way back to prosperity."[23]

The cycle of innovation begins with people who have a basic education and a foundational baseline of skills and competence. If we don't have enough people prepared with the basic education required to create and support the implementation of new ideas that solve new problems, we won't get off the starting block.

When we consider what we do to systematically prepare our people for success, all eyes turn toward our education system … and we don't like what we see.

CHAPTER 3

The Education Issue(s)

"Human history becomes more and more a race between education and catastrophe."

H.G. Wells

E ducation is the bedrock of our country (albeit a bedrock that is decaying) for two basic reasons. First, it provides the fundamental skills required for productive contribution: communication, problem-solving, and foundational knowledge of the basics of how our country works. Second, it's a pre-requisite for accessing the entry-point for many careers and fields. It provides the knowledge, skills, and *opportunity* to participate in the economy, *where the learning cycle continues.*

As we seek to re-start our engine of innovation, it's clear that the solution will be found within our people—and doing what we can to position our people for success is the most important thing we can do as a nation. And the way we're doing that today does not seem to be working. In a March 2010 survey by Zogby International, fully 78 percent of those surveyed believed our schools are failing to adequately prepare children for the high-skilled jobs of the future.[24] Rey Ramsey, president of TechNet, an organization of CEOs from the technology sector, summarizes the issue: "Simply put, all Americans are concerned about the economy and now view innovation as a fundamental kitchen table issue. Most citizens also understand that we may lose our innovation leadership if we fail at basic tasks such as educating our students for the jobs of tomorrow."

It seems like the complaints about our education system have been around forever. As the fiery education reformist and chancellor of the New York City Department of Education, Joel Klein, quips, "In any field but ours, if you fell asleep 50 years ago and woke up today, you wouldn't recognize what's going on. In education, if you fell asleep and woke up today, you'd still be having the same discussions."[25]

The seemingly obvious conclusion is that we must "fix" the education system. The logic is straightforward: as more people receive more education, our workforce will have a higher percentage of educated and skilled workers, which means we'll have more people prepared to innovate and to support innovations—especially in the very important growth areas of science and technology. Therefore, the logic follows, if we invest to improve the education system and funnel more people through it, innovation (and growth, and prosperity) will follow. Sounds reasonable, right?

Well, if improving the education system holds the answer, we need to understand what it is about the education system that's not working.

Why Is Our Education System Failing?

We used to be the world leader in educating our population—what changed? Almost all education experts agree that the systemic challenges in our educational system are both broad and deep. And while there are a seemingly infinite number of opinions on what, exactly, should be done, there is a near consensus on the two most problematic results of our system's failure: 1) too many people are opting out of the system and not receiving the baseline level of education required to be productive contributors to society, and 2) even those who navigate their way through the uppermost echelon of our higher education system are not graduating with the skills employers require for success in the global economy.

Opting Out of Education

America has been the world's most educated nation for centuries—but that is no longer the case. Today, the National Center for Education Statistics (NCES) reports that 30 percent of all high school students drop out, and nearly 50 percent of those who graduate high school do not complete a college degree.[26] As a result, only one-third of the U.S. population is college-educated—which, according to international comparison research commissioned by the non-profit organization Jobs for the Future, puts America in 10th place among our global competitors.[27] Their report goes on to say that the United States is also among the lowest ranking countries in the difference in attainment rates between youngest and oldest workers, which indicates other countries are accelerating the rate at which their young are obtaining education, while America has seemingly hit a plateau.

In September 2009, the NCES estimated that, over the next 10 years, college enrollments will only increase 13 percent (to 21 million) despite the fact that the U.S. population is projected to grow by 14 percent.[28] In *The Race Between Education and Technology,* Harvard professors Claudia Golden and Lawrence Katz sought to understand how these education trends might be related to the growing disparities between upper and lower classes in the socio-economic strata:

> "The sharp rise in inequality (of the last several years) was largely due to an educational slowdown … Our central conclusion is that when it comes to changes in the wage structure and returns to skill, supply changes are critical, and education changes are by far the most important on the supply side. The fact was true in the early years of our

period when the high school movement made Americans educated workers and in the post-World War II decades when high school graduates became college graduates. But the same is also true today when the slowdown of education at various levels is robbing America of the ability to grow strong together."[29]

The good news is that this disheartening situation is getting attention from many great minds around the world. The Lumina Foundation, one of the world's leading higher-education policy institutions, has put a stake in the ground: its high-priority goal is to increase the number of Americans who receive post-secondary credentials from 36 percent to 60 percent by 2025.[30] This "double the numbers" goal is also shared by the Bill and Melinda Gates Foundation, a primary funding source supporting innumerable schools and educational non-profit organizations. The mission of the Gates Foundation: "Help ensure greater opportunity for all Americans through the attainment of secondary and postsecondary education with genuine economic value."[31] This issue is also top of mind for the Obama administration, which has cited its specific intention to increase the number of community college degree recipients by 5 million to "provide Americans of all ages a chance to learn the skills and knowledge necessary to compete for the jobs of the future."[32]

And the increased attention has led to some significant strides forward in access to higher education. According to a study by the Educational Testing Service, there was a significant increase in the percentage of workers with at least *some* level of higher education between 1973 and 2000 (from 28 percent to 59 percent), as well as increases in the percentage of workers who have completed college and earned a bachelor's degree (which jumped from 9 percent to 20 percent during that same period).[33]

However, that is not nearly good enough. The U.S. Bureau of Labor Statistics has identified the 271 jobs with the highest growth potential over the next decade, 100 percent of which require at least some college education—and most of them require one or more college degrees.[34] That means the vast majority of our people aren't qualified to fill those jobs. As David Brooks of The New York Times points out, this is very, very serious. "America's lead over its economic rivals has been entirely forfeited, with many nations surging ahead in school attainment ... the skills slowdown is the biggest issue facing the country...this slow-moving problem, more than any other, will shape the destiny of the nation."[35]

So why are so many people opting out?

Sticker Shock

On the surface, there is an obvious, well-documented, and well-understood financial barrier to following the education pathway to the finish line and obtaining a college degree. The rising cost of college tuition has not only been outpacing inflation for decades, but it's also been rising faster than any other major component of the Consumer Price Index as reported by the American Institute of Economic Research—more than housing, more than healthcare.[36] With an almost inconceivable increase of 248 percent (in real dollars) between 1990 and 2008, the average cost of a degree from a four-year private school—tuition, room, board, and books/supplies—is now a jaw-dropping $35,636, and each year more and more schools join the "$50K Club," as Tracy Jan of The Boston Globe refers to the schools that cost more than $50,000 per year to attend.[37]

The National Center for Public Policy and Higher Education reports that to pay for a college degree from an average four-year *public* university, the median American household would need to invest 25 percent of its total annual income (and the poorest families would need to invest as much as 55 percent of their income).[38] As Tamar Lewin of *The New York Times* concluded in her attention-grabbing headline, "Higher education may soon be unaffordable for most Americans."[39]

What is causing tuition to spike so quickly? It seems logical to surmise that tuition is going up because the costs to run schools are rising for some reason. This "rising costs" rationale for tuition hikes turns out to be true, but only in a small minority of cases. Among the highest echelon of private schools, competition among schools is increasingly driven by which school has the coolest, most modern new facilities. As the perceived baseline of services required for schools to stay competitive has increased, the spending required to deliver those services has ballooned. It's a matter of great debate whether or not these increased costs are really necessary, or if the schools are causing self-inflicted harm by spending more than is needed to deliver value to the market of education consumers. But either way, as the institutional spending has increased, the costs have been passed along to students in the form of higher tuition.

What's interesting is that, in the vast majority of the higher education marketplace, rising costs to run the schools are *not* the issue. Jane Wellman, executive director for Delta Project on Postsecondary Costs, Productivity, and Accountability, noted in her 2009 report, *Trends in College Spending*, "For public institutions over the last fifteen years, the primary reason tuition has gone up has not been because the institutions are spending a lot more money. It's because states have reduced the public subsidies, and colleges are responding by shifting [the burden of covering costs] to students rather than by cutting costs."[40] In fact, the State Higher Education Officers reported that state funding of subsidies per full-time higher education student hit a 25-year low in 2005.[41]

Tuitions haven't been increasing because of rising costs, they've been increasing because schools are asking students to cover a higher *percentage* of the costs. So what happened to the money that used to help cover the costs and subsidize tuition, thereby alleviating the cost burden placed on the backs of our students?

Basically, the states simply have fewer dollars to go around. As the economy has suffered, tax revenues have fallen, reducing available government investment in public services like education. And as costs outside the education market have increased (by having to fund bailouts, for example), the funding going toward education has fallen, and the cost burden has shifted to the consumer.

Although federally funded Pell grants previously covered more than 80 percent of an average public university tuition bill, today those scholarships only cover about a third of the average cost—which means students must find other means to cover the bulk of the tuition costs themselves.[42] Requiring individual students to fund the bulk of the cost to educate our population is new—and represents a largely unprecedented change in how the American workforce gets educated.

Our kids are literally paying the price ....

It's More Than the Price Tag

Our challenges with education are not solely related to the price tag. The high cost is a deterrent only to those who are either unable to obtain financing to pay the costs, or unable to realize a return on that investment. One could argue that, in an efficient market, the appropriate price to charge is the maximum price the customer can (and is willing to) pay. Given that so many consumers are still somehow able and willing to bear the burden of increased costs, doesn't that suggest it's still "worth it"?

According to Claudia Goldin and Lawrence Katz in *The Race Between Education and Technology*, college graduates earn nearly 70 percent more than non-graduates, and the existence of a $1 million lifetime earnings increase for those who go to college (vs. those who don't) is so often cited that it's practically considered gospel.

The wide gap in salaries by level of education has persisted for centuries and is evident around the world. According to the U.S. Bureau of Labor Statistics, the investment in education can be directly translated into incremental earnings. In 2005, Ph.D.s earned an average of $1,421 a week. Those with a master's earned $1,129. A B.A. earned $937. Those with some college (but no degree) earned $653. High school graduates earned $583 and high school drop-outs earned just $409. It seems to be a perfect correlation: more education, more earnings.

However, more-recent data suggests that perhaps the game has changed.

As students have been required to bear an increased cost burden, they have had to find alternate sources of funding to help them pay the increased tuition, and that funding has frequently taken the form of student loans. The College Board reports that over the past decade, student loan debt more than doubled—from $44 billion to $90 billion.[43]

In 2003, the Department of Education published an audit of all student loans taken out in 2000. "Default rates for students across all 4-year schools averaged 19%; 2-year students averaged 30%; and for-profit college students 44%."[44] Defaulting on loans can be devastating to a student's career prospects, given that employers use credit checks as a criteria to evaluate candidates as part of the hiring process. Kevin Carey, of the think-tank Education Sector, offers this sharp insight: "Default rates are where the rubber meets the road ... If students can't pay back their loans, then by definition they are not getting sufficient value for their money."[45] [Emphasis added—and I would have used 2,000-point font if the publisher had let me.]

That leads to a lot of questions that grow increasingly uncomfortable for the ivory tower. With respect to the costs of education, we are reaching a difficult inflection point. Quite simply: are the costs of a four-year college degree (particularly one from a private university) worth the lifetime returns from that investment?

The assumption has long held that a bachelor's degree is a ticket to a higher salary and a higher lifetime income. But with the increasingly larger drag on income that comes from paying off tens of thousands—or hundreds of thousands—of dollars, does the college graduate's lifetime income still surpass that of the high-school graduate who begins earning money sooner, gets a head start by developing hands-on experience four or five years earlier, and avoids the need to pay down crushing student loan debt?

The truth is, the answer to this question doesn't matter—because it's the wrong question. The most important calculation to assess the return on investment in education can't be measured one person at a time.

The ROI of EDU

Much of the battle over education is focused on the individual and whether or not he or she has the means to acquire an education—which is becoming more difficult with the increasing costs that are pushing college beyond the reach of vast numbers of Americans.

When a single student decides to pursue a college education (or not), we could argue that we should let market forces prevail and let that student determine the ROI. If it's "worth it," the student will pay, and if not, the student won't pay. However, when vast numbers of Americans opt out of education, *all of us pay.*

If an educated workforce was "optional," we could let it play out as a rational consumer marketplace dictated by supply and demand. If we had time on our side, the right answer might be to follow economists' advice and let market forces determine the right answer, with Adam Smith's "invisible hand" naturally identifying whether or not the investment in education is truly worth it.

But let's not kid ourselves—the individual cost of a single person's education is only one component of the ROI calculation. The cost incurred when the vast majority of Americans are not sufficiently educated has a price well beyond that of tuition. The full cost also includes taxes we'll all pay to support non-contributors within our society, as well as the cost of lost opportunity suffered by a society that doesn't benefit from the prosperity created by innovation. If too many people don't (or can't) pay tuition, we will all pay in the form of a reduced standard of living.

The primary beneficiary of a single prepared worker is the individual, but the benefits of a prepared *workforce* are shared by all of us. In fact, it's not a big stretch to consider the availability of a prepared workforce to be an issue of national security, or to consider investments in education as important as—and perhaps more important than—ensuring an infrastructure of safe roads and bridges. (If we don't find a way to resolve the looming shortage of air traffic controllers, all the pavement on Earth won't make up for the loss of our air travel system.) If we don't build an infrastructure that puts an educated labor pool in place, our entire economy will stall.

So when it comes to cost, it's not really the price of tuition that matters. It's the cost of not having an educated workforce that we must worry about. Because that's when innovation suffers. And without innovation, there can be no prosperity.

Will More Education Mean More Innovation?

Educating people competently, thoroughly, and continuously from an early age creates a tremendously beneficial cycle for society—to a degree. At some point, however, the value of additional education stops—because the incremental costs are so high that the relative return on investment of an additional year of schooling, or taking an additional class, or adding an additional major, does not create enough upside to justify the additional cost. At some point, you're better off investing your time earning wages and work experience, not more credentials.

The key is not how much time you spend in the classroom—it's how much what you learn increases your ability to contribute. For example, if you do not know how to read, the value of staying in school and learning how to read is enormous—the relative return on the investment to acquire that new skill is tremendous. However, how would you assess the value of spending more time in school to develop the ability to read in Latin?

The way-too-easy trap to fall into is taking on a debate about which topics are "worth it" and which ones aren't. That debate is a fool's game because it completely misses the point. Beyond the essential and elementary subject matter topics of reading, writing, and arithmetic, to a large degree the topical subject matter being taught *doesn't matter*. It's the development of higher-order cognitive skills—like the ability to think analytically or solve complex problems—that matters. And those skills can be taught within any subject-matter topic: learning a new language, composing music, reading classical literature, or studying technology. The pitfall so many fall into is claiming that studying "marketable topics"—like how to write software code—is somehow more valuable than other subject matter areas. That claim is full of holes. First, it's clear that a wide array of talents are needed for a robust economy—even software companies require talent with skills beyond just writing code. Second, the technologies currently taught in school are bound to change at lightning speed—rendering today's lessons virtually obsolete tomorrow.

And as the rate of change accelerates exponentially, the specific topical knowledge being taught matters less and less. The most important thing isn't that we learn today's technology methods—it's that we learn *how to learn*. Accumulating facts and figures isn't the point—being able to think, adapt, and solve new problems in new ways—over and over—is the point. That's what it takes to innovate. And having a workforce that's able to innovate is the point. It is arguably the *only* point.

Once an education has provided a student with the baseline skills (which *should* happen during K-12, but all too often doesn't), the *primary* purpose of further education is to prepare and encourage people to innovate. Putting philosophical arguments about the meaning of life aside, the economic return on investment in higher education *only* exists to the degree that it makes more innovation possible.

The real problem is that what we, as a society, need from our education system has changed—and the system needs to adapt. The problem has evolved, and the job required to solve the problem must evolve, too. Much like the debate in healthcare, the real question isn't about how to reduce the cost of the current system. The issue is that the system doesn't work anymore—and is in desperate need of innovation.

CHAPTER 4

Learning the New Game—and Playing to Win

"If I had asked customers what they wanted, they would have said 'a faster horse.'"

Henry Ford

The threshold for supporting innovation is rising, so the baseline education needed by each citizen to participate in the labor market is rising as well. For example, those who do not know how to use a computer or leverage the information available on the Internet are at a marked disadvantage. They are prevented from even participating in the labor market—even in the most basic jobs (and the jobs requiring the lowest level of skills are most at risk for being replaced by technology).

However, empowering our workforce to achieve a baseline level of competency is not the goal—it is a *prerequisite*. That's why getting as many people into an education system that can effectively teach a baseline level of skills is vital. But it's not enough. It will not achieve the goal.

Leadership in innovation is the goal—because it's only by leading innovation that true competitive advantage, growth, and prosperity can be achieved. Without leadership, America will regress to the global mean socio-economic standard of living. For developing countries, achieving the global mean is a step up. For America, it would be a significant and painful step backward.

The Stakes are High

John Kennedy famously noted that a rising tide lifts all boats. But the converse is equally true: an ebb tide can lower all boats. The collective failure to properly prepare and educate our people comes dangerously close to initiating a death spiral from which it could become extraordinarily difficult to extricate our country. Here's what that death spiral might look like:

- Our nation's businesses begin to find that the graduates of our education system are ill-equipped to fulfill the demands of jobs they need to fill. The employers' options: either fill the jobs elsewhere, stop growing, or devote their own money to remedial training of their newly hired talent. When they decide to invest in training, it increases their costs, and thereby reduces the amount of compensation they can offer all employees (which reduces every employee's income and also the tax base used by our government to fund social investments). The increased costs incurred by employers also reduce the amount of profit and returns companies offer investors, which slows the availability of further investment capital and the jobs that would have been created by virtue of those investments.

- The elapsed time that goes by as new employees are trained is not recoverable. While new hires are trained to become productive and competitive, competitors around the world use that time to pull ahead and defeat American companies in the global marketplace.

- Since American companies are unable to successfully compete, the number of companies declines, and the number of open jobs dwindles. New graduates (and all citizens) have fewer chances for employment and less income to pay down their education debts.

- When education loans default, lenders stop lending at affordable rates, and future borrowers begin to question the value and affordability of an education—so many opt out.

- As more opt out, companies can't hire the qualified people to fuel their growth—and they must spend more money to train more people to contribute. And so on, and so on, and so on.

This hypothetical situation sounds eerily close to home, doesn't it? The question of where the problem starts is a 'chicken and egg' type of riddle. It's not clear where the cycle starts and which breakdown causes the others to breakdown, too. While we once enjoyed a virtuous cycle of innovation leading to jobs and jobs leading to more innovation, today that cycle is breaking down at many different points, with sobering results. The problem starts with the education system—but it is *not only* an education problem.

And as dire as this death spiral sounds, it is not inevitable—there *is* a way to turn this around.

Step No. 1: Ante Up—Get the Basics Right

The first prerequisite is to bring more people up to the baseline level of skills in reading, writing, and math. Again, this is not the goal—it is a prerequisite. It is merely the ante to the innovation game. Like a high-stakes poker game, if you don't pay the ante, you can't play the game. You don't even get a seat at the table.

It starts with the basics, and our system of providing basic education needs help. The National Assessment of Educational Progress (NAEP), also known as the "Nation's Report Card," conducts testing that all states must participate in to comply with the No Child Left Behind initiative. It's intended to serve as an independent, non-partisan measure of our progress in improving educational attainment of students across our country. The findings review the basic proficiency of students in four basic skills and also compares results of various cohorts: white students, black students, Hispanic students, and low-income students. The results of our eighth graders in 2007 are horrifying: in reading, math, science and writing, only 40 percent of the white students tested were found to be proficient. In all the other cohorts, the results were even worse: less than 18 percent were proficient in these fundamental skills.[46]

These results are extremely troubling, not just because so few of our children are achieving proficiency in these basic subjects, but also because even achieving the basic skills won't be enough to compete in the rising high-skill, high-wage economy. People who don't achieve this baseline have no chance. Carlo Rotella of *The New Yorker* interviewed U.S. Secretary of Education Arne Duncan, who understandably expressed deep concern. "The stakes are so high. Education predicts disparities in life chances, outcomes, life income, and the disparity has never been starker. I do absolutely see the dividing line in our society is about educational opportunity, more than around race, even though the two are obviously related. Educational opportunity increasingly divides the haves and have-nots, who's contributing to society and who's a weight on society."[47]

Not only are we failing to achieve our own standards, we are falling behind compared to our international competitors. While research conducted in the 2003 Trends in Mathematics and Science Study reported that U.S. students in fourth and eighth grade scored above the international average, by 2007 our 15-year-olds were ranked 36th in science and 35th in math among 57 countries participating in the Programme for Student Assessment conducted by the Organization for Economic Development and Cooperation.[48] Even more disturbing: even our *highest*-achieving U.S. students underperformed compared to their international peers.

The area where this preparation deficit gets the most publicity is in the STEM (Science, Technology, Engineering, and Math) arena, where the deficits in K-12 competence continue to be evidenced even among the most highly educated students. Today, more of our college students graduate without training in the hard sciences and analytical disciplines. In fact, the U.S. is now

20th out of 109 countries in the percentage of 24-year-olds with a math or science degree.[49] And it's not hard to understand why.

It is a philosophical position among many in the education system that "teachers of all subjects are worth equal pay"—despite the fact that the skill sets required to effectively teach certain subjects, like math and science, have a different (and higher) market value in the world outside a classroom. This means that schools lose the competition for talent as qualified mathematicians and scientists pursue other, more highly compensated, career paths (and who can blame them?). The result is that not only do we have a significant shortage, but an alarming number of teachers assuming the responsibility for teaching our children math and science are ill-prepared. In several states, most high school math and science teachers have never studied math or science themselves. As Richard Ingersoll, professor of education and sociology at the University of Pennsylvania, notes, "High-profile reports from groups such as John Glenn's Commission on Mathematics and Science Teaching for the 21st Century, the National Academy of Sciences, and the National Research Council have all directly tied teacher shortages to the quality of math and science education and, in turn, to the future well-being of the economy and [even] the survival of the nation."[50]

Our country is essentially "winging it" when it comes to reinforcing successful methods for developing these critical skills among our children. As Kathleen McCartney, dean of the Harvard Graduate School of Education, wrote in an editorial published in *The New York Times*, "The United States has 14,000 school districts making individual decisions on curriculum, standards, and assessment—in contrast with other countries. No wonder American high schools rank 25th in math and 21st in science on international tests."[51]

She goes on to highlight the additional complication that the people running school boards are often elected officials whose only experience in education is derived from the fact that they were once students as well. Essentially, our country is betting its future on the hope that 14,000 distinct governing boards each invest the time, resources, and focused attention required to successfully improve our methods to develop math and science skills. There isn't a bookie in Vegas who would take that bet.

But as we saw in the K-12 NAEP results, it's not just in math and science where we're failing our students—it's in the basic fundamentals of reading and writing, too. And there's more. American students also failed in a special assessment of problem-solving skills, ranking 29th out of 40 participating countries. Cognitive skills have been demonstrated to be significantly more important in determining economic outcomes than any specific measure of school attainment. As the Organization for Economic Cooperation and Development (OECD) points out, "Increasing the average number of years of schooling attained by the labor force boosts the economy only when increased levels of school attainment also boost cognitive skills. In other words, it is not enough simply to spend more time in school; something has to be learned there."

Step No. 2: Playing to Win—Creating a *System* of Innovation

Getting more of our people through an education system able to arm them with the baseline of essential skills is a crucial first step. It's necessary, but not sufficient. Once we "ante up" and enter the game, how do we play to win?

Low test scores and insufficient graduation rates are certainly troublesome. But what is perhaps even more disturbing is that the ultimate customers of our higher education system—the employers who hire our college graduates—are not happy with the results of those who make it all the way through.

Companies are experiencing the problems of educational ineffectiveness firsthand. Employers who hire college graduates (even those who have received the full dose of "education" prescribed by our education system) complain that new entrants too often don't know and haven't been taught the right things. And their complaints run the gamut from "students aren't being trained in the most current technology languages," to more general basics like "they require too much attention and feedback."

Almost any manager can share horror stories about appalling oral and written communication skills that are, at best, embarrassing and, at worst, a significant inhibitor of global business. Incoherent sentences, "TXT-speak" e-mail messages, and credibility-damaging documents that fail to comply with basic grammar or punctuation—they're a daily fact of life in every organization. Even basic workplace rules and etiquette—such as punctuality, appropriate attire, and interpersonal communication—are often completely foreign to entry-level hires.

A collaborative survey of 400 employers by the Conference Board, Partnership for 21st Century Skills, Corporate Voices for Working Families, and the Society for Human Resource Professionals found that "professionalism/work ethic, oral and written communications, teamwork and collaboration, and critical thinking and problem solving [are] the most important skills that recently hired graduates from high school and two- and four-year postsecondary institutions need."[52]

Too many students graduate without these key skills—which means that despite their years of schooling and training, even our most highly educated workers are considered unprepared to fully contribute to the needs of employers who are the engines of our economic success.

As Jim Spohrer, the director of university programs at IBM, laments, "It's really easy to find people that are 50 percent of what you are looking for...It's really hard to find people who are 90 percent of what you're looking for. This is a real dilemma."[53] Apparently, even IBM's $1 billion-a-year training budget can only pick up so much slack.

Because educators are removed from the front lines in industry, curricula often deviate (sometimes radically) from the topics and skills that employers require on the front lines and drift to subjects that are not deemed valuable to employers.

The rapid rise of so-called "for-profit" education companies (known in the past as trade or vocational schools, or by their more modern moniker, "career colleges") is evidence that solving this training problem means big business. ITT Technical Institute has been the shining star of Wall Street, and CEO Kevin Modany reported annual revenue growth of 30 percent (to $1.3 billion) even during the disastrous economic meltdown of 2009.[54] Their success has been driven by their ability to take the burden of practical training off the shoulders of employers. The emphasis of the programs taught by the likes of ITT, Devry, Kaplan, University of Phoenix and others is on providing students with "applicable knowledge"—the ability to learn the specific skills that employers need to fill today's open jobs. While these schools make an important contribution toward solving the problem, we're still just scratching the surface.

Remember, knowledge that's known today isn't really the main point. To innovate, the more important issue relates to being prepared for what's coming next. A study by *The Economist* found the top three skills expected to be in demand by employers over the next decade were life skills, problem-solving skills, and leadership—while traditional skills such as science, math, or written communications ranked far lower.[55] The ability to continuously apply new thinking to new problems as they evolve over time—and to do so again, and again, and again—that's what really counts. Knowing isn't the main point—it's the ability to learn and adapt that matters. According to Robert Zemsky, an education professor at the University of Pennsylvania and author of *Remaking the American University,* "We've got to move away from talking about a fixed knowledge base that is anything but fixed, and talk about ways of accessing that knowledge base over a period of a lifetime."[56]

It is time to sound the alarm. If we agree that prosperity comes from innovation, and innovation comes from people, we should also agree that we need a systematic way to prepare and encourage our people to innovate—and the tailspin our country is in right now is ample evidence that whatever we're doing now isn't working.

Companies and industries that rely on well-educated, well-prepared professionals are increasingly forced to take matters into their own hands because our education system isn't supporting the kind of developments our economy needs.

Are We Teaching the Right Things?

It's unclear if the materials taught within our education system align well (or at all) with what's needed to support innovation in today's global economy.

When asked how to assess schools on the basis of their ability to prepare graduates for success in the real world, Bob Morse, research director at *U.S. News & World Report*, responded, "We're constrained by the data available. Currently it's not possible on a comparative basis to measure outcomes or learning or student engagement or what is really going on in the classroom."[57]

Even among our most prestigious higher-education institutions, some of the most basic analytical skills required for after-college success are largely absent. As Tara Siegel Bernard suggests in *The New York Times*, "For a country that prizes personal responsibility, we're doing very little [to prepare our children with basic financial life skills]…Most Americans aren't fluent in the language of money. Yet we're expected to make big financial decisions as early as our teens—Should I take on thousands of dollars of student debt? Should I buy a car?—even though most of us received no formal instruction on financial matters until it was too late."[58] The Council for Economic Education reports that only 13 states require students to take a course related to financial or economic principles, and there are only 34 states where it's even possible to take those classes (because those topics have been approved within their curriculum guidelines).[59]

"Financial illiteracy among students and adults has been well documented by countless surveys," says Robert F. Duvall, president and CEO of the National Center on Education and the

Economy. "And as our [data] tells us, the reason for this is no mystery: what isn't taught isn't learned. It's as simple as that." These practical basics aren't even taught to our most advanced students; no *wonder* we're facing a financial crisis when most Ivy League colleges allow students to graduate without any exposure to basic accounting.

Our education system is focused on academics. But true preparation also includes the ethic, spirit, and associated skills of innovation—entrepreneurship, problem solving, ideation, adaptability, and the ability to synthesize ideas and concepts. That's not a course. It's not a major. It's something that gets infused throughout one's way of thinking, working, and learning. That's what we must aspire to teach.

Today, more than any specific skill, companies want employees who can adapt—because, as the saying goes, change will be the only constant. They want people who can think and learn quickly. The curriculum that's needed is less concerned with what facts a student knows, and far more concerned with passing down the ability to think and contribute—that's what will truly unlock each student's potential. Employers can't predict the future or how the skills they need will evolve. But we know that the problems will evolve—and the jobs to solve those problems will evolve, too. Are we teaching our students how to evolve?

Time for New Tactics?

Maybe the issue isn't *what* we're teaching but *how* we're teaching. Perhaps the familiar (but outdated) paradigm of "research, review, write, publish, and then teach" is no longer an effective way to share knowledge. Furthermore, perhaps the act of transferring knowledge is no longer sufficient to accomplish what we need from the education system. In fact, the entire model seems to be a vestige of a time when communication was much slower. In today's networked, high-speed world, that model is simply too lethargic to fuel our competitiveness. The tactics employed by our education and learning system must adjust to a new world for us to remain competitive and thrive.

In her recent *Fast Company* magazine cover story, "A is for App," Anya Kamenetz describes remarkable uses of technology to teach children—inside and outside the classroom.[60] She describes Seth Weinberger and his innovative new product, TeacherMate, as presenting the "tantalizing prospect of revolutionizing how children are educated by drawing on their innate hunger to seize learning with both hands and push all the right buttons." And the results are remarkable—using the student-specific, game-like software to help a teacher provide unique lessons on each child's learning station and receive real-time feedback on their performance, teachers can let each child learn at his or her own pace and easily know when and where a child might be getting stuck and need guidance.

Kamenetz goes on to describe Paul Kim, chief technology officer at Stanford University's school of education, and his efforts to take it a step further—empowering kids to teach themselves. Kim found that, when given access to TeacherMate, students from all across the world—from Mexico to Rwanda—readily explore and learn on their own. "With these devices, what the kids pick up in two minutes, the teachers need hours to learn," Kim says. "They're so innovative ... Why does education need to be so structured? What are we so afraid of?"

Who's on First?

OK, maybe the problem isn't *what* we're teaching or *how* we're teaching but *who* is doing the teaching. There is much debate about the way in which we hold our teachers accountable for their performance. In a recent *Newsweek* cover story, Evan Thomas and Pat Wingert suggest that, "The key to saving American education is [to] fire bad teachers."[61] They point out that, after two or three years, many teachers receive lifetime tenure, which insulates them from accountability in a way not found in any other profession. They go on to celebrate Rhode Island superintendent Frances Gallo, who famously fired every one of her school's 74 teachers when they refused the request to spend more time with students and be evaluated by a third-party. The debate over the basic competence of our teachers rages across the country. As of 2000, 37 percent of all teachers came from colleges with SAT scores in the lowest 5 percent of the nation—and many believe that unions are to blame because they will do just about anything to protect their members from being fired.

In his controversial article in *The New Yorker,* Steven Brill quoted a New York public-school principal saying that Randi Weingarten, the leader of the 1.4-million-member American Federation of Teachers union, "would protect a dead body in the classroom."[62]

While I am absolutely in favor of holding teachers accountable, I think there's a different question we should ask: is it even reasonable for us to expect teachers to do the teaching? The fact is, the people who've chosen a career path in the classroom are *not* on the frontlines of our economy. The new knowledge is coming from the labs, from entrepreneurs, from innovators. Expecting teachers and professors to be solely accountable for this transfer is unreasonable. They don't have the knowledge themselves, and the rate of change is extremely fast. How can we expect teachers to be the purveyors of this rapidly expanding body of information? They are not on the frontlines—they are in the classrooms!

Our traditional education system *was* an entirely appropriate approach for its time—when there was no Internet, no jet travel, no e-mail. It made complete sense to have a series of steps and processes that were linear and sequential. Now? It makes no sense. Today, we must deal with discontinuous ambiguity—the unproven, unprecedented, fast-changing, and unpredictable modern world in which we live.

Who's on the front lines in this new world? Entrepreneurs. Researchers in corporate R&D labs. Certainly, universities continue to be another hotbed of innovation. What can our nation do to enhance and accelerate the flow of ideas from these professionals?

Unfortunately, the skills we need and the knowledge that's emerging from the new generation of innovators are not always effectively rippling their way back into the education system. There are few courses, for example, in "business model development" or "renewable energy" at most colleges and universities. We must become faster and better at this—and simply teaching it faster might not be enough. The new game requires *learning* faster.

But ... what if we're looking at this all wrong?

If Henry Ford had asked his customers what they wanted, they wouldn't have said they needed a car—they would have asked for a faster horse. Within their view of the world, using their familiar frames of reference and perspectives, they were unable to conceive of a different solution—or to even to recognize how the problem was evolving. They didn't need a faster horse, or even a car for that matter—what the world needed was an exponentially faster way for citizens to get from Point A to Point B.

Maybe, just maybe, we're looking at this entire situation through our old and familiar lenses and missing the whole point of what's really going on. Maybe the issue isn't *what* we're teaching, *how* we're teaching, or even *who* is doing the teaching. Maybe the fundamental problem is that the problem itself has evolved—and we are looking at the problem in the wrong way, using old thinking that no longer works.

As Albert Einstein famously pointed out, no problem can be solved with the same thinking that created it—and although the crisis we're facing is enormously complex, one thing is crystal clear: we are in *desperate* need of new thinking.

The underlying assumption we hold of our "education system" is that it's *us* educating *them*. The entire premise assumes that we know something they don't know, and we need them to learn it. What if that isn't the full story? In fact, what if we have this backwards? What if *they* know something we don't know—and we need *them* to teach *us*?

And there is hope ….

Something very interesting has been building over the past two decades. While we have let our country slide into its current crisis, a new generation has been growing up—coming of age while it watched the damage being done on live, 24/7 news channels. From 1978 to 2000, a new generation was born—"Generation Y"—and they see the world very, very differently than the rest of us. Their perspective is unlike any other because they use an entirely different lens, one that was custom-crafted during the unique timeframe in which they came of age. Their new perspective may be exactly what America needs to get back on track; they have the ability to see the new problems in new ways and identify new ways to solve them, which is exactly what's needed to kick-start our engine of innovation. Their ability to lead the way with fresh ideas and new thinking may hold the answer to whether or not America as we know it will prosper—or even survive.

America is on the brink ... and Gen Y has arrived on the scene just in time.

CHAPTER 5

Our Secret Weapon: The Right Team at the Right Time

"No problem can be solved from the same level of consciousness that created it."

Albert Einstein

"Generation Whine"—that's how some insist on characterizing the cohort of nearly 100 million people born between 1978 and 2000. It's the most entitled generation, the most isolated and disconnected generation, the "trophy generation," the offspring of "helicopter parents," and the generation with the largest gaps between expectations and reality.

Whether it's "Millennials," "Generation Y," or "Echo Boomers," you've heard all the stereotypes and clichés before. This new generation is needy—unsatisfied with merely occasional feedback and constantly seeking affirmation and approval. Their Gen X and Baby Boomer predecessors complain that they have a negligible attention span, they are disrespectful and self-righteous, and that they seem to think using correct grammar is somehow beneath them. Ouch.

In my career, I've enjoyed a unique vantage point—helping to bridge the gap between higher education and the working world. For the past 14 years, I've been able to observe this remarkable group of people and gain some insight into their goals and aspirations. What Gen Y really is, in my opinion, is the most *misunderstood* generation in history. Even their monikers are off-base. Gen Yers don't relate to any of the labels bestowed upon them (but for the record, they seem to consider the term "Millennials" to be the least offensive because it hints at the breakthrough potential of a new era). There's a canyon-sized gap between what they're known for and what this extraordinary generation is really all about.

A (Very) Brief Overview of Generational Distinctions

Before we zoom in to examine some of the tired clichés, let's look at why this generation is so different. While I'm not eager to embark on some type of anthropological tourism, I'd like to put my observations and assessments of Gen Y in the context of what it means to be a "generation" in the first place. [Please note: *extensive* research has been done to document and understand generational differences, and I have included many great sources in the back of this book for your reference.]

For a variety of reasons (some well-understood, some ambiguous), well-demarcated generations emerge every few decades. They arise from shared circumstances that are notably different from the experiences of the previous generation. It's important to understand that generational break points are not defined by parent/child relationships—siblings can be from different generations as well. For example, although only seven years separate me from my twin brothers, they are members of Gen Y, while I am Gen X. We, and our sister Melissa, all grew up in the same house, on the same street, with the same parents, and went to the same schools, but our perspectives have been shaped differently. One of the biggest differences in our life experiences? My brothers *grew up* with access to computers, while I was first introduced to an Apple Macintosh at Dartmouth College. The differences that mark generations as distinct from one another are derived from the *common experiences* shared by a cohort and the ways in which those experiences shape their collective worldview.

Boomers remember where they were when JFK was shot. For Gen X, the photo of Christa McAuliffe and the lost astronauts aboard the Space Shuttle Challenger brings us all back to a pivotal and vivid moment. For Gen Y, there have been a myriad of seminal events—ranging from Columbine to 9/11 to the historic election of President Barack Obama. Members of each generation develop attitudes, values, and a shared perspective of "social norms" that, in turn, create the sense that they have more in common with one another than with those in other generations.

Baby Boomers, of course, loudly and aggressively separated themselves from the protective bubble of the 1950s nuclear family (to the evolving soundtrack of Elvis, the Beatles, and Jimi Hendrix—though no one wants to take responsibility for the Bee Gees, it seems...). The rebelliousness shared by those in the Boomer cohort was, perhaps, a predictable reaction to the protectiveness and triumphant successes of Tom Brokaw's "Greatest Generation." Those coming of age in the 1970s were aptly described as the "Me Generation" for a good reason. Today, however, that self-centrism has mellowed and evolved into ambitions for second or third careers. It's been replaced by an insatiable desire to transform how their generation ages, and by a refusal to subscribe to the traditional conventions of their parents.

As Boomers reached their childbearing years, they often parented in non-traditional, hands-off ways. Their children—so-called Generation X—looked at the landscape and didn't actually seem to rebel, *per se*. Left on their own and assumed to be capable of figuring things out for themselves, these "latchkey kids" did exactly that. They retreated into MTV and Atari and developed a relentless desire to respond to hands-off parenting through zealous independence. Their attitude: "We've survived just about everything else you've thrown at us—we'll survive this, too." Don't tell a Gen-Xer what to do. He'd much rather figure it out for himself—and by himself. But now, with Gen Y, we're seeing a completely different picture.

Given the challenges facing our country and the world, Millennials have ample opportunity to test their mettle. And if they can lead us out of the tailspin we've created for them, maybe they'll earn a new label: the Innovation Generation.

What's so great about Gen Y?

Gen Y is different than the rest of us. And I would argue that the new perspectives, the new values, and new thinking that Gen Y brings to the table are exactly what we need to solve the challenges facing our world today. The *Gen Y Way*, as I refer to it, represents a new worldview—and one that all the rest of us can learn from. From my perspective, the following are the fundamental components that make up the **Gen Y Way**:

- **G: Global**—In their worldview, perspective, and scope, Gen Y sees things from a broader vantage. Their lens spans a wider point of view.

- **E: Experiential & Experimental**—Gen Y learns by doing—in iterative, interactive ways that are rich in discovery and feedback loops.

- **N: Networked**—More than any previous generation, Gen Y is intensely and inherently connected. They're the first generation with networked technology in its classrooms, homes, and cars—everywhere. And they learned to use the newest technologies *before* their parents did.

- **Y: Why Not?**—Gen Y respectfully challenges old thinking and assumptions.

- **W: Winning Is a Team Sport**—It's a generation that's seemingly wired to collaborate, ask for help, and work in groups and teams. To them, the game is all about "we," not "me."

- **A: Action**—There's a palpable sense of urgency in Gen Y, a desire to stop passing the buck and dive into action. They didn't create the many problems we face, but they know it's on their shoulders to come up with solutions.

- **Y: Yes, We Can**—Don't be fooled into thinking this is just a dated, partisan political slogan. There's a reason this motto resonated with so many young voters: because Millennials consistently rally around the belief in what's possible.

GEN Y WAY: Global

Like no generation before it, Gen Y understands the scope and scale of the multi-faceted problems we're facing. They've been raised within a global economy, informed by a global network of 24/7 information and news. They've been sensitized to ever-present concerns about war, climate, genocide, and hunger—issues that are increasingly less abstract because our world has become smaller through technology.

Millennials are sometimes written off as superficial or disinterested, but I don't see them that way at all. Today's world is a totally different place. Previous generations waited a day to read a news story printed on paper or perhaps put dinner on hold to watch a news broadcast from the "Big Three" networks. Those were the available choices.

Now, just 20 years later, those information constraints seem almost as quaint as the horse and buggy. Today, Gen Y is used to and comfortable with selecting from hundreds of cable television channels such as CNN, Fox, MSNBC, CNBC, C-SPAN, and more—all splashing news stories 24/7, on television, online, and on their cell phones. If that's not enough, they can get news stories from any of dozens of news aggregators or check Twitter for real-time reports—anywhere, anytime, all the time. The result: Gen Y has a much stronger sense of what's going on in their world than previous generations could ever have hoped to achieve.

More than any previous generation, Millennials are also globetrotters. Thanks to less-expensive and more available travel options, Gen Y has seen more of their world—inside and outside the country. According to a recent study by Zogby International, 56 percent of 18-to 29–year-olds had family or friends living outside the U.S.—no other cohort in the study even came close.[63] And where they haven't traveled, technology has provided an unprecedented level of exposure and access through cheap long-distance, global broadband, and 24/7 rich-media access. It is not unusual for elementary school classrooms to use Skype to connect—via live video and voice connection—to kindred classrooms on the other side of the world. Goodbye pen pals, hello global classmates.

Gen Y's global awareness is enhanced by the significantly higher levels of education that they can access and complete. Three to four generations ago, in an agrarian, early-industrial economy, a high-school diploma was the exception. Today, a scant 60 years later, a bachelor's degree is essentially the minimum table stakes for a career—and in many fields, a master's degree is virtually a minimum requirement.

While there are many, many challenges in U.S. education, there are successes, too—and accessibility is chief among them. Millennials don't need to be in a classroom to access the most cutting-edge knowledge. Today, the materials for nearly every course offered by the Massachusetts Institute of Technology (MIT) are available online (http://ocw.mit.edu), and they're *free*. What's more, Millennials have been raised by parents with higher levels of education—parents who have created a richer intellectual home environment that values academics and rewards scholastic achievement. When they were younger, these parents enjoyed access to CD-ROM encyclopedias and online libraries. Now, Wikipedia and Google and an almost limitless range of educational resources are available through the Web.

The overall result: a generation with a broader global perspective and awareness than any prior generation. Their global outlook plays a critically important role in how they're able to provide the new thinking so desperately needed for innovation. Today's problems are sophisticated, global in scope, and are evolving quickly—and we need global thinkers to find innovate new solutions.

GEN Y WAY: Experiential and Experimental

Gen Y learns in ways that are distinctly different compared to Gen Xers or Boomers, embracing a (not surprisingly) action-oriented, iterative approach. With so many simultaneous tasks and information flows coming and going at such a fast pace, Millennials are accustomed to higher levels of (often quite nurturing) feedback at far more frequent rates. And it's no secret that this particular characteristic has become a famous point of contention as older generations see it and label it as neediness or a lack of independence.

What gives rise to that thirst for experiential learning? I think it's tied to the fact that Millennials are the generation that has lived the *uber*-scheduled life. Stand around any soccer field or hockey rink today and listen to the parents' conversations: "Emily has gymnastics at 4 today. Matthew has hockey practice at 6 a.m. tomorrow and two birthday parties..." "...Then we've got book club, piano lessons, Spanish lessons, and math tutoring..." "I hope we can find time to squeeze in a play date for Julie and Meg to get together…"

And if you get those parents in an even mildly candid moment, they'll quickly admit, "No, my parents never did anything resembling this kind of thing for me. It was mostly: 'Go outside and play with your friends.'" Social commentators might decry a generation of overly managed kids—and there's validity to that concern. But I believe that potential downside is offset by an important upside: this generation is now far more comfortable with a packed agenda, competing priorities, and conflicting demands.

At many of my speaking engagements, this topic of style comes up often and usually precipitates an overflow of latent, sometimes visceral, frustration. "It's like they've landed from another planet," one executive lamented recently. Millennials have been raised at a different pace and with different goals. Their motivation is to get better, contribute the most, achieve a personal best—and continue to progress from there.

They have greater appreciation for guidance and input from the people who've done this before. They ask questions because that's how they've built relationships with their elders—seeking advice from the many coaches in their lives who have helped them learn. They thrive on direction and feedback, which is admittedly different from Gen Xers, who aggressively seek a go-it-alone independence.

It's a mistake to confuse their eagerness for input with a lack of initiative, or an inability to pay attention or take in detail. Instead, I view it as an ardent desire to ensure a better outcome. Gen Yers are inherently wired to try, seek help and feedback, and try again. Hmmm. People who want to take direction and incorporate feedback to do a better job. Doesn't sound *all* bad, does it?

GEN Y WAY: Networked

Where would Gen Yers be without technology? More than any other, Generation Y is truly the technology generation, and proved it by adopting it faster than the adults who raised them—which is an incredible, revolutionary, and unprecedented dynamic. Throughout history, adults were the first (and often only) ones to access the latest technical advancements. Even well into the 20th century, technology adoption filtered down from the workplace, where adults learned the expensive new technologies as part of their jobs. More recently, price points have brought technology costs down to consumer levels. With access to affordable technology in their homes and the time to experiment, the kids became the experts. They know the latest and greatest. They intuitively know how to use it—and have extended its applicability in new and imaginative ways.

Instantaneous   information   and   communication   have infiltrated every corner of every day, and we've bred a generation of people who are far more comfortable with fast-paced multitasking in highly enriched and stimulating environments. Psychologists will explain that if you're exposed to a lot of stimuli, it can create stress and cloud decision-making. But if you've been *raised* that way, your brain actually develops differently and you're able to adapt faster. Millennials are constantly focused on the next step, the next project, the next goal. Their evolved abilities will serve them well in today's fast-paced, always-changing environment.

Gen Y leverages and relies on technology to form, sustain, and extend relationships of every level and type. From e-mail and voice mail to texting, micro-blogging, and IM, Gen Y is connected to more people than any previous generation. Just think: this is a generation that's been growing up without *any* barriers to connectivity—not even long-distance charges or busy signals. Critics can fairly point out that the outer margins of these relationships are not meaningful. It's highly unlikely that the MySpace or Facebook user with 1,000 "friends" has meaningful relationships with more than a handful of them. But for Millennials, these online tools enable them to forge enhanced connections that are more durable, more immediate, and more frequent. This will have significant ramifications to corporations, whose workforce will be more than 50 percent Millennials within five years. If you agree with Ken Blanchard that "none of us is as smart as all of us," then the Millennials seem to be on the right track.

GEN Y WAY: Why Not?

Gen Y relates to peers and colleagues—and superiors and parents—in different and unique ways. They have a different view of hierarchy and status, and are fearless in crossing organizational boundaries to share opinions with executives who they quickly view more as colleagues than as superiors.

One interesting dynamic concerns Millennials' relationships with their parents. Family experts often note that there's almost camaraderie between parents and their Millennial children. There's more negotiation and consultation in the relationship— less unipolar, prescriptive parenting. This gives Millennials a confidence and a sense that each can learn from the other. They are more open to accepting—*and giving*—input and advice. This type of two-way exchange is radically different from what Gen X or Boomers experienced.

That same dynamic carries over into the college classroom and the workplace. The respect for elders is there, but there is less deference. It's more of a peer/colleague relationship. Millennials are not rebelling *per se* (at least not by Boomers' standards!), but they're unafraid to ask bold questions and engage in healthy debate to work toward a common solution. What's more, we're even seeing the traditional dynamic of adult teaching child being turned on its head as Gen Y takes the lead in teaching elders how to maximize their use of technology.

They're not afraid to simply ask, "Why not?" From their perspective, when they see that the current approach isn't working, the obvious question is, "Why should we continue to do it that way?" While this type of challenge is often irritating to Gen X or Boomers ("Why should I have to explain it to these insubordinate brats? I wish they'd stop wasting my time and just do it!"), what's really happening is not defiance or neediness for attention. When Gen Y questions the status quo, it's because they're looking at the situation through a different lens, and what they see doesn't add up. They see that the old ways don't work— and they can't help but question why we'd want to continue down the wrong path. This type of questioning shouldn't be chastised—it should be celebrated and rewarded! New thinking is the *only* way we are going to find innovative new solutions.

GEN Y WAY: Winning is a Team Sport

More so than their predecessors, Millennials place high value on collaborative teams and interdependence—they prize 'we' over 'me.' Given their complete embrace of unifying technologies for communication and collaboration, it's no surprise that there's a stronger sense of "we're all in this together." This, after all, is a Title-IX generation—one that grew up immersed in organized sports—with a strong team ethic.

With Generation X, the term 'Trophy Kids' referred to children who were, in some instances, viewed as accessories and props for high-profile parents who used parenting as an exercise in consumerism—the child was the trophy.

With Gen Y, that same term has taken on a more sardonic tone. Today, with so many children participating in so many sporting events, every kid gets his/her own 'Participation Trophy'—and some skeptics and cynics see it as rewarding mediocrity.

Has the concept been taken too far? Perhaps. We certainly can't, and shouldn't, shield children from the undisputed truth that competition produces winners and losers. But there's value in this approach, too. It reinforces the concept that *your personal best* is and should be the goal in every effort you make. That's become a starting value and cardinal principle for Generation Y. It reduces the pressure of "*I* need to beat the other person" and creates a climate where "We can *ALL* be successful." In a world where complex solutions require collaboration and compromise, this ethic will be vitally important.

This ties into a social-mindedness as well. To a Gen Yer's way of thinking, doing the right thing by society is NOT in conflict with doing the right thing for yourself. After growing up with so many vivid examples of fraud and corruption—where greed and excess have been exposed and rejected—Generation Y has an uncommon passion for social contribution. They've heard loudly and clearly from even the winners in capitalism that financial success can still leave a gaping hole in the soul and an unmet need for fulfillment.

For those of us who came of age in earlier generations, the temptation is to softly chuckle, exchange a few sidelong glances, and mutter, "Wait 'til they start making mortgage payments and have children." Fair point, perhaps. But Gen Y does not view economics and cultural values as distinctly different spheres. To Gen Y, these realms are highly correlated and connected. Millennials have seen the extremes—the Enrons and Worldcoms, the Bernard Madoffs and other titans of greed and fraud. And they've largely rejected that option. They're not anti-capitalist—but they are definitely anti-monopolist, anti-fraud, anti-unfair. When 'shareholder value' gets expressed as the ultimate goal, Millennials instinctively recoil.

Research consistently shows that wealth is not everything, or the most important thing. Increasingly, money is viewed by Millennials as a practical tool to enable them to pursue their other goals and passions.

So what *does* matter to Gen Y? Life experiences. Friendships and family. Choices and freedom. A more balanced life. They want the opportunity to have and be mentors and role models. And they want a never-ending opportunity to learn and grow. This generation brings the concept of being a "team player" to a whole new level.

GEN Y WAY: Action

Whether it's a book-sharing program, adopting a sister school in Africa, tutoring underprivileged kids, or raising money for healthcare research, Gen Y has moved our society from vaguely aware to motivated to act—not simply out of idealism, but out of a renewal of the shared values that are woven throughout the fabric of our country. It's born of the American Dream: the sense of entrepreneurship, possibility, accountability, and self-starting. There's something in the Gen Y fabric—a sense of something larger than themselves, a sense of community and connectivity— that is, frankly, refreshing after too many decades in which these values have seemed to atrophy. Gen Y wants the freedom and ability to pursue a higher purpose and larger mission.

Millennials want to see how their work makes a difference. They want to see the opportunities that lay before them in their organizations. In fact, many HR experts point out that a visible career path and development plan serves as a critical retention tool for Millennial employees. Gen Y wants to work with organizations that have more than a cursory commitment to community service and social improvements. This needn't be politically based (although that approach is certainly valid and appeals to many).

With Gen Y, there's a sense of ownership of the key issues we face as a society. And with that ownership comes a time-sensitive imperative. They are not going to wait for someone else to fix the problem. In fact, after watching years or decades of political gridlock and high-volume/high-octane arguments on cable channel after cable channel, their experiences to this point have bred a strong skepticism of previous generations' willingness or ability to fix the problem. They know that the problems have evolved—and that the job to solve the problem has evolved, too. The old ways don't work. Old thinking won't work. To Gen Y, the need for new solutions couldn't possibly be more obvious. For Gen Y, it's time to stop talking, stop bickering, stop promising— and start *taking action*.

GEN Y WAY: Yes, We Can

"Yes, we can." It's more than an overused or outdated political slogan (and, as recent events have shown, political momentum can be an awfully ephemeral phenomenon). This tiny turn of phrase perfectly captures the resilient energy born of an enduring optimism. Yes, Gen Y brings a youthful exuberance to the table—and, yes, that's a requirement for success. But it's not sufficient—simply nodding and smiling and repeating an affirmative mantra won't get the job done. We need more than aspirations and slogans—and fortunately, there's something inherent in the background and makeup of Gen Y that makes them uniquely suited to *sustaining* that enthusiasm through a self-perpetuating cycle of *optimism-action-optimism-action*.

The common traits and characteristics of Gen Y create an important overarching belief: the strong sense that they can do things differently and better. Ultimately, these millions of Millennials have a remarkably different worldview that shapes their approach to diagnosing and solving challenges. Collectively, these and other characteristics uniquely position them to rise to the occasion for our country.

My strong sense is that the people in this newly emerging generation are not merely *capable* of responding to the many-fronted challenge of the next 50 years. They are *ideally suited* to this particular moment. They know that a better world is possible and worth pursuing. They can sense their significant place in history—they know it's up to them, and they know they can do it. And, lucky for us, they're not taking "no" for an answer.

CHAPTER 6

Closing the Innovation Gap: New Thinking + Experience

"What use could the company make of an electric toy?"

Western Union, when it turned down
rights to the telephone in 1878

It is quite possible that history would have taken an entirely different course if Bill Gates hadn't crossed paths with Dr. H. Edward Roberts.

Dr. Roberts is widely credited with being the inventor of the personal computer. He was the innovator who first introduced the MITS Altair, the world's first general-purpose microcomputer—and he was the mentor who gave Bill Gates and Paul Allen their start. The software they wrote to run on Dr. Roberts' machine, Microsoft Basic, was the first product of what would become the world's largest software company. When Dr. Roberts passed away in April 2010, Gates and Allen released a joint statement to remember Dr. Roberts and to recognize the impact their mentor had had on their lives. "Ed was willing to take a chance on us—two young guys interested in computers long before they were commonplace—and we have always been grateful to him."[64]

If Gates (who was a student at Harvard at the time) and Allen (who was a young up-and-comer at Honeywell) hadn't been prepared for the opportunity to help Dr. Roberts, the opportunity wouldn't have taken place. But it's also true that if Dr. Roberts hadn't exposed Gates and Allen to the new MITS Altair and given them the opportunity to apply their new thinking, then that, too, would have prevented the innovation from occurring. It was not just that Gates and Allen were ready for the challenge—it was also that they were *introduced* to the challenge. This is the two-part recipe for innovation.

Farming vs. Fusion

The national discourse on education is all about teaching students something that *we* know, and *they* need to learn. The same type of language is usually heard when employers talk about hiring entry-level talent or offering students internships. The premise is that the employer-to-entry-level-hire relationship is like farming: the employer needs to plant seeds and then work hard to create the best conditions to raise those seeds into crops. Training and mentoring serve as fertilizer and water, giving the seeds of new talent the nourishment they need to grow. And it's not until the seedlings have fully grown that the farmer earns a return on these long-term, time-intensive, laborious investments.

But this charming line of thinking is emblematic of the old thinking that has caused so much trouble for our country. Farming isn't the right conceptual model. A much more applicable analogy to use would be cold fusion … and here's why:

When fusion occurs, two atomic particles come together and connect, creating unimaginable—and, to a large degree, unpredictable—energy as a result. What's more, as Scott Chubb explains in the science magazine *Infinite Energy*[65], the study of cold fusion (which is the term for fusion that occurs at room temperature, rather than the high temperatures normally required to create nuclear fusion), is progressing more slowly than necessary because scientists have been slow to believe the mounting body of evidence that it's actually *possible*.

The type of fusion we need in America is the combination of new thinking with the problems that need to be solved, and the people who have the resources and power to bring new solutions to life. Innovation is a two-step process: it not only requires people who are prepared with a baseline level of education, but it also requires that they have the experience to see the new problems that need to be solved—and have the opportunity to apply their new thinking to invent new solutions.

The fact is, you can't learn to ride a bike by reading about it or watching someone else. You can't learn to play the piano by studying. You have to actually get out there and ride the bike and practice the piano. We need to make hands-on pragmatics a core component of our national curricula. And to do so, we must close the large gap between education and the working world.

The Great Divide

For the last century or two, there has been a fairly rigid division between academia and industry. You went to school where you were taught by professional teachers for a variable number of years. Then you entered the working world where you interacted with an entirely new cohort of colleagues. But those two worlds have never effectively collaborated, and it's been this way for far too long. This separation between education and the working world—this gap between theory and action—is one of the fundamental reasons why we find our country facing numerous persistent challenges on so many fronts. And it poses a significant threat to our engine of innovation.

How we prepare our young people for workplace success is a key area of conflict, pitting academic education against hands-on, pragmatic learning to prepare for careers. It's a dispute that has endured, and the businesses of tomorrow and their future employees are caught in the middle.

On one side of the debate some argue that higher education offers an irreplaceable opportunity for young people to explore and discover and should not be poisoned with what they perceive to be "job training." They emphasize that liberal arts academics play an important role in our education hierarchy, and that a 21st-century curriculum must maintain a prominent place for classic literature, arts, philosophy, foreign languages, history, social sciences, and other disciplines that have elevated mankind for centuries.

On the other side of the debate are those who see evidence of an unprepared, unproductive workforce—and employers who are unable to fill jobs because a qualified talent pool is unavailable. As *Business Week* reported in April 2009, despite that fact that the U.S. unemployment rate rose toward 10 percent, more than three million jobs went unfilled because our workforce lacked the necessary skills.[66]

Our academic culture has long eschewed—and, in some quarters, actively disdained—educational curricula that focus on hands-on training for professions and careers. It has been derided as little more than trumped-up trade school. That view is deeply misguided and represents a big part of the problem: the perception that this is somehow an "either/or" choice. We must not allow ourselves to continue this foolish debate any longer—it is a false choice.

Academic topics are not in conflict with 21st-century skills— they simply represent the arenas in which the skills related to innovation can be taught. To teach problem-solving, critical thinking, and the skills essential to innovation, the topical subject matter doesn't matter all that much—these skills can be incorporated into almost *any* subject matter. It's not *what* students know—it's that they know how to think, learn, and apply new thinking in new ways.

A 21st-century curriculum can and should have ample room for both worlds to coexist. An integrated curriculum should teach people how to think and how to act on that thinking. Both traditional academics and experiential learning can do this very effectively—*even more so* when they are well-integrated. Mounting evidence suggests that practical learning *accelerates* academic results.

In a world of rapid change with global communication and commerce, yesterday's classroom education alone is not enough. When students graduate without the skills needed for innovation, there are serious ramifications: companies spend too much time and money (individually and collectively) providing the hands-on education—the "training and development" that are needed to create a productive workforce. This becomes a hidden tax on profitability. As Donna Klein, the executive chair of Corporate Voices for Working Families, acknowledges, "It's a losing strategy for employers to try to fill the workforce readiness gap on the job. They need to be involved much sooner to prepare new employees to succeed."[67]

As we get employers connected to the education system, we must do so carefully—in a way that doesn't detract from or potentially corrupt pure academic research. No one would support a model that calls for all academic research to be directly funded by commercial enterprises. The risks of conflicting motives are too great and readily apparent.

Instead, we must integrate industry in a manner that complements and supplements academics in parallel and coordinated ways. Let's get role models in the classrooms who bring pragmatic insights, cutting-edge thinking, and practical applications of new knowledge. Our ability to innovate will depend on our new thinkers being exposed to the new problems on the front lines. We must bridge the gap and close this great divide. Today, the gap seems to be widening—and the bridge is out.

The Bridge Is Out: Career Services

Bridging the gap between the education system and the working world is mission-critical. It's the best and fastest way to create the 'fusion' between the new thinking of Gen Y and the new problems needed to be solved. The challenge is that the bridge we depend on to connect these worlds and carry the weight of this responsibility is fragile and weak. Today's model for bridging education and the working world is broken. The college career centers that we rely on to shepherd our students into the working world are fundamentally set up to fail.

Serving the competing and conflicting needs of students, employers, faculty, parents, alumni, and administrators, career services personnel valiantly try to achieve the nearly impossible. With a decreasing pool of resources, they must engage more students, create more programs and resources, deploy software and services, work alongside more employers, aggregate job and internship leads, and streamline an inherently inefficient process.

Too often, college career centers are viewed as little more than a small team of counselors who double as event planners, scheduling on-campus recruiting, a few career fairs, and maybe some discussion panels with alumni or prospective employers. Based on that traditional model, the typical center usually consists of a dozen or so overtaxed staff members attempting to serve an average of 5,000 students—plus the employers, alumni, faculty, parents, administrators, state governments, and other constituents who helicopter in when they need something. (And their needs usually take the form of data and reports to document how many graduates have been placed into jobs at that moment in time.)

The notion that a handful of administrators and career counselors can effectively support all of the individual needs of students and grads is deeply flawed. Imagine, for instance, if those same 5,000 students received all of their classes from just 15 faculty members. Even the most talented counselors can't support so many clients using yesterday's tools: counseling sessions, job-posting databases, career fairs, on-campus recruiting, and other small-scale programs. Providing informed career advice to students requires knowledge of the world's evolving industries, companies, and job types. To expect career counselors to keep up with the rapidly changing complexity of the modern world is not simply unreasonable, it's preposterous. There has to be—and there *is*—a better way.

A new approach is desperately needed. While some colleges have recognized the value of devoting greater effort to making their career centers more efficient, most have dealt with institutional budget cuts by reducing investment in non-academic functions, and trimmed their "non-core" career service budgets even further. On some level, these budget cut decisions actually make perfect sense—because all the budget in the world won't fix the broken model we have in place. We don't necessarily need more spending, but we *desperately* need new thinking.

The real need extends far beyond the efficiency of the career center staff. The real need is to improve the *effectiveness* of the career development *system*, and to build a strong, effective, sustainable bridge between the education system and the working world. The problem has evolved and the job of the career support system has evolved, too.

When the game was "finish your education first and then enter the working world," the old model may have sufficed. However, if we are going to fuel innovation, we need to harness the power of fusion. We need to connect our new thinkers with the front lines—and waiting until they're "done" with their education won't benefit them or us. We need a better way to bridge the gap so the connections happen sooner and in more meaningful ways. The evolved job of career services isn't just to counsel or to place students in jobs. It's to create *connections* among new thinkers and the new problems being solved in the working world.

In my view, schools and businesses must do far more than close the gap. They must do more than merely meet in the middle. They must overlap—significantly. Going forward, a cross-functional collaboration will improve education and work output and position our country for much better performance in the decades to come.

Two-Way Exchange

According to Paul Krugman, the 2008 Nobel Memorial Prize winner in Economic Science, "If there's a single central insight in economics, it's this: There are mutual gains from transactions between consenting adults…If the going price of a widget is $10 and I buy a widget, it must be because the widget is worth more than $10 to me. If you sell the widget at that price, it must be because it cost you less money to make it. So buying and selling in the widget market works to the benefit of both buyers and sellers."[68] In other words, exchanges don't happen unless both sides win.

Too often, when employers consider hiring Millennials and have the old-thinking 'farming' analogy in mind, they question the benefit they're getting from the exchange. "I don't have the management time to run an internship program," a division manager of a large media company recently confided to me. "It's just too much work to invest the time, energy, training, guidance, coaching—you name it—just to have all that investment walk out the door."

It used to be that college graduates joined a company right after school and were trained over the course of a 30-year career. The return on investment by employers to train new apprentices was obvious. The more they prepared their employees for success, the faster, larger, and better their employees' contributions to the company's success would be. Companies gained the full upside of their investment via a lifetime of contribution from the people they groomed. Today, that game has changed.

According to the U.S. Bureau of Labor, college-age employees change jobs an average of every 18 months.[69] A recent Experience survey found that many employers don't even expect them to last that long.[70]

With a wider variety of options—and increased mobility— young workers don't have to make lifelong career decisions at an early age. They can try new jobs with new companies, build their hands-on experience, and get a better sense of their personal preferences and working styles as they develop. While this type of flexibility may be great from a personal-development perspective, it creates a perception among employers that it's too costly to invest in new employees. For one of my clients, it costs more than $14,000 to find and recruit a new entry-level hire— and more than $100,000 to replace her if she quits. Painful.

But is retention really the right way to assess the value of Gen Y hires? To some degree, of course, retention matters. When an employee (at any level) leaves, the company suffers through direct replacement costs, distractions, lost productivity, and lost time. I would argue that, while these costs may seem steep, the cost of *not* investing in Gen Y talent is much, much higher—because without Gen Y hires, companies can't benefit from the new thinking that is so desperately needed for innovation.

New Thinking In Action

To give you a sense of what kind of upside is available when organizations adopt the 'fusion' mindset and bring the new thinking of Gen Y into their organizations with gusto, let me share just a few examples.

In early 2005, NASA began to pay closer attention to the writing on the wall—the talented men and women staffing America's air and space programs were reaching retirement age, and there weren't enough young people to backfill the looming vacancies.[71] To begin to shore up their talent pipeline, they created a new internship program to bring a few dozen students into the fold. They'd start with these interns, build an understanding of what it takes to run internship programs (which was new to many of the line managers who had spent their careers focused on the science of space, not that of human or organizational behavior), and build from there.

As the director of education programs at the Kennedy Space Center shared during a conference on workforce development, many of the seasoned veterans weren't particularly enthusiastic about being asked to "babysit the youngsters," as they saw it. But the rocket scientists followed management's request, and one of the engineers responsible for the Space Shuttle was in the process of giving a tour to the squad of interns when he discovered the power of fusion.

The NASA engineer was explaining how the Shuttle design was being re-engineered to be more powerful, while using less fuel. It was a big challenge because, with so many sophisticated and interdependent parts, any change made to one area of the Shuttle would undoubtedly have ramifications for the design of all the other related components—so the iteration process was intense. As the student interns took in the information, they began tossing around ideas among themselves (typical of Gen Y), and speaking up to ask a series of "why" questions (also typical of Gen Y). "Why is the team working in a serial process to iterate?" "Why don't the team members work in the same building?" "Why does the Shuttle need more power?"

If you are Gen X or a Boomer, your blood might be starting to boil as you sense the frustration this world-renowned scientist probably experienced as he answered each question one by one (while simultaneously watching the clock tick toward his afternoon deadlines). In exasperation, he told the interns that he'd answer this last question and then they'd need to move on—and he quickly rushed through a brief explanation that the reason the Shuttle needed more power was to carry the additional weight of new technologies being brought to the International Space Station. As he got up to usher the interns to the door, one of them lobbed in a last question just under the buzzer: "Why do you *paint* the Shuttle? Doesn't that add weight?"

With that simple question, NASA had discovered the value of Gen Y's new thinking. At that moment, the issue of whether or not they'd retain the interns after their summer stint became much less important. The investment in the interns had already paid off as NASA saved millions of dollars with that single idea.

OK, that may have been just a lucky guess. Fresh ideas come "from the mouths of babes" all the time—and we all sometimes miss seeing the forest for the trees when we're too close to the problem. That's not necessarily specific to Gen Y, right? Fair enough. So let's try this example on for size…

Across Africa and much of the Middle East, Zain is the leading telecom provider, serving more than 72 million subscribers and recording more than $8 billion in annual revenue. While the 22 countries Zain serves are diverse (spanning Saudi Arabia, to Kenya, to Morocco), the company identified a key strategy for success that is common across all their markets: targeting the "youth market," and the 18- to 25-year-old consumers who represent 50 percent of the population.[72] It was the market opportunity these young people represented that originally set Zain down the path that ultimately delivered staggering results.

The "FUN" program began three years ago in Jordan. The Future University Network was originally intended to help Zain understand the mindset of the customers they wanted to target. Students from all majors were hired into a program that mimicked the working world—a virtual company that included positions in marketing, sales, product development, customer care, and other functional positions. The intent was to give students hands-on work experience while also giving Zain the opportunity to learn about their styles, habits, and preferences.

What Zain found was that these students picked up the skills they needed much faster than expected, and they began building out their own IT infrastructure, developing their own performance management programs, and even creating their own stock option plan to share ownership in the student-run organization. They also found new revenue streams. Furthermore, the students created a "train the trainer" model by which current students in the program train the new hires—and between the highly efficient and productive model and the increased revenue generated as a result of ideas from this program, the entire effort became self-funded.

Building on the success of the students in Jordan, Zain took it a step further. When the company entered the Bahrain market, Zain was the third entrant—late to the game. The CEO, Dr. Saad Al-Barrak, decided to staff the entire Bahrain office with Gen Y talent. His reason? "They are fresh and fearless people." They are also innovators. With 80 percent of the staff of the Bahrain division coming from Gen Y, Zain has built one of the fastest-growing, most highly profitable divisions in the entire company. In its most recent annual financial statements, Zain reported that the Bahrain division delivered $56.9 million in net income, the sixth-highest producer of all 22 countries Zain serves—and they were able to deliver these results despite the fact that Bahrain is among the very smallest countries on the list.

Today, there are 215 students in the Jordan program—Zain hired six from the program last year, "the cream of the crop," according to Zain management. They have created a self-sustaining method for recruiting the very best talent while also delivering real business gains. That is absolutely brilliant—even more so because Zain is not the only winner in this new game. With a certificate from the Zain program in hand, program graduates are highly attractive in the talent market and are often hired by other companies at higher levels in the organization than they otherwise would have been. And, as Dina Saad, director of Youth Programs, points out, "In Jordan, the problem is that companies want to hire people with experience, but students don't have experience, so it's hard for them to get jobs—this is the dilemma ... We are helping to solve that problem for Zain, and for all other companies, too."

Do you think it was 'beginner's luck' that allowed these students to build a leading telecom division in a market where they were the third market entrant? Clearly, they couldn't have done it without the support of Zain's visionary leadership and resources—but that's the whole point. Both sides of the equation are needed to win the new game. The global perspective, technical savvy, and collaborative approach so central to the *Gen Y Way* made this group of innovators uniquely suited to solve this problem and achieve success. This isn't just youth bringing fresh perspective. This is a sign of well-prepared, tech-savvy, team-oriented innovators bringing new thinking to new problems. And when their new thinking was combined with visionary leadership that applied their new thinking to new problems and supplied the resources to bring the new ideas to life, what happened? Innovation. And success.

Still not convinced? Believe me, there are *a lot* more examples where these came from ....

When the pollsters evaluated the odds of a little-known senator from Illinois beating a world-famous, *uber*-connected former First Lady in the race to become the Democratic presidential nominee, it seemed he didn't have a chance. So much of politics is momentum, and the funding required to promote the platform of a new candidate can easily exceed tens of millions of dollars before the campaign even begins.

In 2007, during the lead-up to the primaries, the machinery of the Barack Obama presidential campaign was well underway. Historically, the results of the Iowa caucus, in particular, had been seen as a critical "must win," and all of the very experienced and talented political strategists were focused on how to introduce Obama's message to the voters in that state. But looking at the problem from a new perspective, Chris Hughes, one of the twenty-something co-founders of Facebook, saw the possibility of a different approach.

Rather than focusing on broadcasting Obama's message to voters, Hughes saw it the other way around: allowing voters to feel heard might be a better way. And furthermore, connecting with the new perspective of the up-and-coming Millennials required that the Obama campaign relate to the *Gen Y Way*—collaborative, networked, action-oriented, global in scope, experiential … the typical and tired old ways of campaigning weren't going to resonate.

Hughes was the mastermind behind My.BarackObama.com, the website that is largely credited with being the most powerful secret weapon in Obama's winning arsenal. The easy-to-use networking site was used by the campaign not only to communicate Obama's platform, but to also help supporters create groups, organize events, collect campaign contributions, and stay connected with one another. By the time Obama moved into the White House, volunteers had used the site to create more than 2 million profiles, help 35,000 groups manage 200,000 events, and raise $30 million.

Ellen McGirt of *Fast Company* magazine interviewed David Plouffe, Obama's campaign manager.[73] According to him, "Technology has always been used as a net to capture people in a campaign or cause, but not to organize. Chris saw what was possible before anyone else." McGirt goes on to explain that, "Hughes built something the candidate said he wanted but didn't yet know was possible: a virtual mechanism for scaling and supporting community action. Then that community turned around and elected his boss president."

By seeing the challenge in a new way, Hughes was able to see a new way to solve it. And he did so in the face of old thinking. "I know I ruffled feathers," Hughes told McGirt, but he realized, "there was no way I could walk into David Plouffe's office and say I'd need 10 people. He'd say, 'What for?' And I'd say, 'To create a national grassroots infrastructure of peers.' And he'd say, 'How is that going to help us win Iowa?'"

New thinking was required to see how technology could create new possibilities and tackle big challenges in new ways. But it was just as important that the new thinkers were given the chance and resources to make it happen. Hilary Clinton's team had the support of many Millennials, too—but on her campaign team, it was the seasoned experts who ran the show. They were relying on tried and true methods and old thinking—and the results speak for themselves. Innovation requires new thinking.

Think about that for a moment: new thinking and the *Gen Y Way* put the leader of the free world in office. *That's* the power of fusion, and what's possible when new thinking is combined with the experience of tackling new problems. That's innovation, the *Gen Y Way.*

CHAPTER 7

Innovation
is a Team Sport

"The measure of who we are is what we do with what we have."

Vince Lombardi

For generations, we've been culturally fascinated with entrepreneurship. From John Rockefeller and Henry Ford to Steve Jobs and Bill Gates, we've seen how the right people in the right circumstances can create unprecedented prosperity for vast numbers of people. But let's be clear: these entrepreneurial superstars did not achieve success by themselves. They had the opportunity to apply their new thinking to new problems and access to a prepared workforce ready to help them bring innovations to life.

Another commonality among innovators? They have mentors—people who encourage their new thinking and give them the opportunity and the resources to apply their new thinking to important problems at need solving. By having *exposure* to the new problems, the *preparation* to understand them, and the *opportunity* to apply their new lens and new thinking to invent new solutions, innovators have the opportunity to innovate. The recipe for innovation requires new thinking *and* experience.

The source of new thinking is people with new lenses—a new way of thinking that provides new perspective, not perspective that is trained to be just like ours. Companies that do this well win. Countries that engage their young in the workforce win. Not because we train them, but because *they* train *us*.

If we are to solve the major problems facing our nation and our world, we must prepare our people to be problem-solvers. We must prepare them to innovate by solving new problems in *new* ways. The old ways of thinking will not work. Band-Aid attempts to address the situation (read: trillion-dollar stimulus plans that our great-grandchildren will be paying for) may restore near-term confidence and get some people back to work temporarily, but they will not solve the root problem, which is that we are not giving our young people the opportunity to combine their new thinking with experience.

Bridging the Gap

Some visionary companies—with various motives ranging from profitability to altruism—have recognized the value of new thinking and are attacking the problem with new and innovative approaches. They see the shortages of skilled graduates. They know that new thinking is imperative for innovation. And the best part? They're taking action. Here are some examples of steps being taken to close the gap between education and the working world, and those who are leading the way forward by example.

➤ *Microsoft: Students to Business*

As the world's largest software company, Microsoft has not only led the way in personal computer technology, it has also expanded into a wide range of new markets. From servers and storage solutions for businesses to video game consoles and digital music players for consumers, Microsoft has consistently pursued innovation. With its recent launch of the sophisticated search engine Bing.com, Microsoft has taken on its biggest rival, Google, in a head-to-head battle—and has proven yet again that it has the DNA to adapt and deliver new solutions that solve new problems in new and better ways.

To achieve continued success in such a highly competitive and fast-changing arena, Microsoft has had to innovate repeatedly—and has also had to ensure that its partners, the hundreds of thousands of companies that build and use software that runs on Microsoft platforms (such as Microsoft Windows, Microsoft

Exchange, or even the Microsoft Xbox), have what they need to succeed as well. In the world of software, the ecosystem is absolutely essential for success. The more programs that are available to run on Microsoft platforms, the more consumers and businesses want to use those platforms, and the more people using the platforms, the more likely new developers will want to build for those platforms. In other words, the more people who have Xbox consoles, the more developers will want to create Xbox games (instead of inventing games for competitors like Sony or Nintendo).

With technology changing so quickly, Microsoft sensed a growing gap between the technical skill sets of college students and those required by employers. If this skills gap led to Microsoft or its partners becoming unable to access enough talent to fuel their growth, the ecosystem would be at risk. So Microsoft stepped in with yet another demonstration of innovation to solve this new problem.

Microsoft's Students to Business program is an inspiring approach to bridging the gap between academia and the working world.[74] A dedicated team at Microsoft brings together more than 600,000 worldwide partners to educate students and prepare them for innovation with free software, free online webinars and training, and access to inspiring role models around the world, Microsoft is working to enhance the skills of the next generation and inspiring them to pursue careers in technology. "As technology needs grow across all industries," says Aimee Sprung of Microsoft, "we're enabling the next generation of technology professionals with the tools, training, and experience needed to be effective in the industry."

What's more, the Students to Business program also connects this young talent directly with Microsoft partners, pumping a large and growing pipeline of new thinking and fresh ideas directly into the ecosystem. By actively encouraging partners to engage up-and-coming talent in projects, internships, job shadows, and entry-level positions, Microsoft is creating the fusion needed to bring new thinking to new problems—and sparking innovation.

➤ Intel: Science Talent Search Competition

In March 2010, Erika Alden DeBenedictis unveiled the software navigation system she invented to enable spacecraft to follow highly efficient paths through space. Building on the NASA-approved Interplanetary Superhighway concept, she invented a method to refine the course of a spacecraft while it's en route, taking into account the gravity and movement of planets to allow for more efficient transit through the solar system. The most incredible part? Erika is only 18 years old.

The Intel Science Talent Search is a national competition that gives high school seniors the chance to develop and present their original research with prominent professional scientists. This year's competition attracted 1,736 high school seniors. Three hundred were recognized as semifinalists, and, of those, 40 finalists were invited to Washington, D.C., to compete for $630,000 in awards, including a top award of $100,000 from the Intel Foundation.[75]

When new thinkers and their fresh perspective come together with role models who can support their efforts and help them apply new thinking to big problems, the results are *stunning*. Projects presented by other finalists included work by David Liu, 18, who analyzed digital imaging to empower unmanned aerial vehicles; Eric Brooks, 16, evaluated genetic factors related to the spread of prostate cancer; and Benjamen Sun, 17, who studied how debris on city streets can lead to contamination of city water sources.

Thomas Friedman, *The New York Times* columnist and author of international best-seller *The World Is Flat,* attended the awards ceremony. "In today's wired world ... just about everything is becoming a commodity, except imagination [and] the ability to spark new ideas," he said. "Gotta say, it was the most inspiring evening I've had in D.C. in 20 years."[76]

➤ *New Model for Career Services: Focus on Connections*

One of the more important—and one of the most overlooked—ways that we can bridge the gap between higher education and the working world is by reinventing the model of career services. By shifting the expectation from a narrow focus on counseling or placement to a broader mission of creating connections that fuse students with the working world, college/university career centers have the potential to serve as a gateway to alumni and other professionals in the working world.

Schools that invest in cultivating ongoing relationships with alumni put themselves in a position to achieve major advantages and differentiation. Those schools enjoy a stronger reputation and brand, leading to higher demand for admissions. This is particularly true and relevant as parents and students demand more ROI from schools before investing valuable time and major tuition dollars.

Most colleges and universities in our country consider career services to be a peripheral, non-core administrative function—but not all of them. There are some shining stars, some innovative leaders who apply a new perspective and new thinking—and they deliver inspiring results.

Laura Denbow is one of those leaders. In 2006, she and her team at the Bucknell University Career Development Center invented what they call the "Bucknell Externship Program."[77] Alumni are engaged every January to host the rising sophomores during the three-week January break. These "externships," as Laura calls them, give her students quick stints with employers—most of whom are alumni of Bucknell or parents of current students—to shadow professionals and get a tangible understanding of how the working world works. She found that not only does this program provide enormous benefit to the students (by giving them valuable insight prior to choosing a major) *and* the alumni who host the interns (by infusing new thinking into the working world), but it also benefits Bucknell. The externship program allows Bucknell to reengage its alumni base and strengthen ties between alumni and the institution. And as any development office will attest, happy, engaged alumni are more likely to donate their time and resources in support of the school.

Innovative leaders at other colleges have begun similar efforts (including Matt Purdy at Southern Illinois University Carbondale, who set up a two-week externship for Randy Lane with our team at Experience in 2010). And these programs aren't limited to colleges, either. At the Governor's School in South Carolina, every rising senior is placed in a six-week off-campus experiential learning opportunity as part of the Summer Program for Research Interns.[78]

The Nelson A. Rockefeller Center at Dartmouth College has created an innovative way to bridge the academic study of public policy with real-world practical experience. The Center's Policy Research Shop offers undergraduates the chance to contribute nonpartisan research to the real policy debates going on in Vermont and New Hampshire. Students meet directly with public officials, conduct independent research related to topics under consideration by the states, and present their findings to legislators. The Center's First-Year Fellows Program take it a step further, offering a summer program that brings students to Washington, D.C., puts them through a five-day "Civic Skills Training" program, and places them in internships with government and policy-related organizations so that they can experience public policy development in action.[79] Experiencing this program together as a team, the students not only learn from their specific internship assignments, but also from each other as well.

At Duke University, Bill Wright-Swadel and his team at the Career Center work with employers to create "simulations"—projects that put students on teams that tackle real-world problems for real-world clients, which range from global consulting firms to government agencies. Recent simulations have included business plan competitions, market research projects, and even new product development efforts.[80] "Collaborating with faculty, the career center aims to support the tandem goals of academic excellence and professional development," notes Wright-Swadel. The goal of these simulations is to create fusion that benefits both sides—students win by developing real-world experience, learning from role models and mentors, and building both their resumes and their professional networks. The employers who sponsor these projects win by accessing new thinking and by getting a competitive edge in recruiting. They're cultivating important relationships with the fresh talent they need to succeed.

"Career service offices can be an extraordinary strategic advantage to their institutions, but only if they embrace change," said Shelia Curran, founder of Curran Career Consulting and author of *Smart Moves for Liberal Arts Grads: Finding a Path to Your Perfect Career.* "A prerequisite is university leadership that values the success of its students and graduates. Given that support, career services offices need to change the way they do business."[81]

The recent hot debate across the higher education landscape concerns the topic of assessment and outcomes—and how to measure the results and performance of higher education institutions. The debate is complex and largely focuses on how to assess the abilities of each student upon graduation. When it comes to assessing the performance of a school in its ability to connect its students to the working world, there's a far simpler way to measure success: count the number of connections made between each student and professionals in the real world. A connection could be defined as a one-on-one interaction between a student and a professional in the working world—whether it's for a work-related project or for professional development.

It's the *count* of connections per student that matters—so much so that it's unnecessary to dwell on the qualitative aspects that determine a "good" connection versus a "bad" one. The fact that the connections *exist* is far more important than any other factor—even suboptimal experiences are still valuable learning experiences. If institutions and their career centers were measured by the number of connections per student—and not the number of jobs posted on their websites, the number of programmatic activities that took place, and the like—we would build a much more meaningful bridge between education and the working world, and students, employers, alumni, educational institutions, and our country would *all* benefit.

➤ NFTE: Get a job? No—make a job.

Another model that has shown remarkable and inspiring success is the National Foundation for Teaching Entrepreneurship.[82] The NFTE works with students from low-income communities to engage them in non-traditional educational opportunities where they can learn entrepreneurial skills by tackling real, hands-on projects that often help local businesses grow. A multi-year longitudinal study led by Professor Michael Nakkula of the Harvard Graduate School of Education found that participating in these hands-on programs increased the students' interest in college by 32 percent—and also increased scores in reading, self-starter initiative behavior, and leadership. Allowing these students to learn by doing—rather than learning by studying—has created breakthrough performance.

In his commentary on "Escaping from Poverty,"[83] *The New York Times* writer Nicholas Kristof reported that efforts by schools to connect students with employers to give them practical work experience delivered long-term results. Eight years of follow-up research shows those kids are more likely to hold jobs and earn more money. And the stories of NFTE alumni paint a clear picture of how innovative, entrepreneurial young people change the world (see the inspiring details at www.nfte.com). From launching T-shirt companies to establishing global mentoring networks, the teens empowered by this program are finding new ways to solve new problems, and using their innovative fresh thinking to lift up low-income communities around the country, and around the world.

At this point, NFTE has reached more than 280,000 young students, and have trained more than 1,500 educators as "Certified Entrepreneurship Teachers." This growing army of innovators will create the jobs that build prosperity for all.

➤ Workforce Development Initiatives: Private/Public Partnerships

There are several areas of our country that are leading the way as models in how to effectively bridge the gap between education and the working world—and proving exactly how much it benefits everyone involved. In Austin, Texas, for example, the links among educated talent, entrepreneurial spirit, government and non-profit support, and corporate success is clear—the virtuous circle is in action.[84] To begin, more than 40 percent of the population has a bachelor's degree. Companies like Electronic Arts, Dell, and Intel are all investing there because of the talent pool. The University of Texas houses the Austin Technology Incubator to support fledgling entrepreneurial ventures. The Texas Emerging Technology Fund provides funding for start-ups. Groups like Bootstrap Austin encourage networking and create the opportunity for fusing new thinking and new problems that need solving. And training initiatives like the government-funded non-profit Workforce Solutions provide training to continually upgrade the skills in the talent pool.

It's also no coincidence that Austin makes extensive efforts to attract young, Gen Y talent to its city. In March 2010, Portfolio.com named Austin the best city in America for young workers. And the results? A thriving economy leading the way in innovation across a wide range of industries—including music, gaming, design, and high tech.

In Massachusetts, similar efforts are underway to attract young, educated talent. The Massachusetts Innovation & Technology Exchange (MITX) has launched a "Recruit and Retain" initiative to promote the growing new-media industry in the state, and to counter the misconception that all "cool" innovation is happening on the West Coast. Scott Kirsner, writer for *The Boston Globe* and author of the blog *Innovation Economy*, reports that many companies—from State Street to Genzyme—are attempting to step up the marketing of New England to attract the up-and-coming talent that is so critically important for innovation and growth.[85]

Jack Wilson, president of the University of Massachusetts, reminds us that "the number one resource for economic competitiveness is talent" and that when academia, government, and the private sector come together to bridge the gap between education and the working world, everybody wins.

➤ FIRST Robotics:
"In our league, all the players get to go pro."

Another program that's caught the eyes of many is FIRST Robotics (http://www.usfirst.org/). Founded by Dean Kamen, National Medal of Technology winner and noted inventor of the Segway, this nonprofit organization ambitiously aims to make science "cool" through a varsity sports model of interscholastic competition. FIRST challenges teams of high schoolers to solve a common problem in six weeks using only a standard kit of parts and a common set of rules. Teams build robots from the parts and enter them in competitions that escalate to a national level. Their mission is "to transform our culture by creating a world where science and technology are celebrated and where young people dream of becoming science and technology heroes."

If you have never attended a FIRST Robotics competition, you are really missing out. The championship event, which this year was held in the Georgia Dome, rivals the Super Bowl—but with *more* energy and excitement. Paul Gudonis, president of FIRST, embodies the passion and commitment behind the organization's mission. He and his team have inspired more than 90,000 supporters to participate as volunteers and mentors to more than 200,000 students—and have engaged more than 3,500 sponsors to contribute their support.

An independent study by the Brandeis University Center for Youth and Communities found remarkable results. Compared to their peers, students who participate in FIRST are not only significantly more likely to attend college, they were also three times more likely to major in engineering, four times more likely to pursue a career in engineering, and 10 times more likely to have an internship during their freshman year in college. They are also more than twice as likely to volunteer in their communities. And, as Dave Lavery, the program executive for solar system exploration at NASA, explains, companies and government organizations involved with the program benefit because FIRST is "creating new engineers who will drive the future economic engine of the country."[86]

That's fusion in action.

➤ *Lockheed Martin: Send in the Boomers*

Lockheed-Martin, the $40 billion defense-technology contractor, creates fusion in a different way. As a high percentage of its skilled workforce began to near retirement age, the company recognized it wasn't just fighting for its *share* of skilled people—there simply weren't enough skilled people to support the *entire industry's* need for talent.

Chief executive Bob Stevens stated, "At Lockheed Martin, we know firsthand the importance of educating our young people in math and science. Our future success—and our nation's technological advantage—depends on a constant supply of highly trained, highly capable technical talent."[87]

Their approach: forge partnerships with public schools to implement high-school curricula that bridge the gap between academia and industry. They are investing real dollars to develop curricula that encourage studies in math and science. The company is training teachers and providing teaching materials, lab experiments, and other tools to help teachers get up to speed and fuel a science-rich education.

What's more, at Lockheed, Boomers who are on the cusp of retiring—people with extensive knowledge—are encouraged to return to college and attain appropriate teaching credentials. Through its educational benefits plan (which has traditionally only provided training for up-and-coming workers), Lockheed pays for those college courses that employees earn while still employed on a full-time basis. This is a model that many companies can replicate and that can deliver enormous value to our economy. As Boomers reach retirement age, we risk losing a generation of institutional knowledge unless we find a systematic mechanism to fuse their experience with our new Gen Y workforce. Lockheed may be pointing the way to one model for achieving that.

Revving Up the Innovation Engine

There is one drawback to these inspiring efforts: non-profit organizations and companies like Microsoft and Lockheed Martin are doing this on their own dime. That's not enough. Altruism and philanthropy isn't a sustainable model. We need to make the education-industry partnership sustainable, which means there must be an obvious return on investment. We need to ensure that there's a measurable, near-term, bottom-line return to accompany the long-term benefit that we all anticipate and envision coming from such initiatives. That's the key to ensuring this becomes a sustainable proposition.

Breaking down the harmful misconception that investing in young talent is like 'farming' instead of 'fusion' is the first step. When the private sector understands that investing in Gen Y talent is in their immediate best interest, it will make a big difference. But what other steps could we take to motivate action?

Uncle Sam: Innovators Need Your Help

In the information age, innovators had access to new arenas of innovation. The innovators were here—in California, Austin, Seattle, and throughout the R&D labs and research facilities of the world's best educational institutions, think tanks, and government-sponsored agencies.

Now consider again where the innovations in renewable energy are taking place: Finland, Singapore, China, and India. In this new era of innovation, what will happen if our most well-prepared talent isn't exposed to the challenges that need new thinking? What happens if our young innovators—who bring with them exactly the right new thinking we need to find new solutions—don't have access and are not exposed to the new problems that need solving because the people working on those problems are elsewhere? Or, even worse, what happens when companies can't be bothered to invest in "inexperienced" young talent? How will our country reap the benefits of new thinking and innovation?

Stephen Ezell of the Innovation Technology and Innovation Foundation explains what's happened. "Over the past decade, many of our competitors—from Great Britain and Finland to Japan and South Korea—have created national innovation strategies designed specifically to link science, technology and innovation with economic growth."[88] These central, national policies connect education, policy development, R&D, workforce training, tax, intellectual property, and digital infrastructure—because it's clear that the only way to win is through coordinated strategies that leverage resources in government, education, and the private sector. To Rui Grilo, architect of Portugal's innovation strategy, it's obvious. "Knowledge, technology, and innovation must be at the core of a country's national economic policy."

Finland has its National Innovation Strategy and a Strategic Center for Science, Technology and Innovation, which is a partnership between schools, companies, and government to guide the innovation agenda for the country. And to complement its innovation strategy, Finland set a national goal to equip 100 percent of its high-school graduates with the technical, analytic, and communication skills it perceives necessary to compete in the global economy. India launched its National Innovation Foundation in 2000. Sweden launched Vinnova in 2001. Thailand created its National Innovation Agency in 2003. The Netherlands launched Senter Novem in 2004. Singapore created Fusionopolis and Biopolis, multi-million-square-foot research centers to attract 10,000 of the world's preeminent scientists to Singapore. Seeing a trend?

The United States used to be a leader in innovation. Even our innovation-related policies were among the most innovative. The U.S. was first in the world to offer R&D tax credits, for example. Today, the U.S. is 17th when it comes to R&D tax credit generosity. When Intel assessed whether to build its new microprocessor plant in America or China, it determined that it could cost $1 billion more to build in the U.S.—and not because of a difference in labor costs. Ninety percent of the cost difference was attributable to government policy differences such as grants or taxes, not wages.

If Uncle Sam doesn't sharpen his focus on innovation-friendly policy, we're going to keep falling behind. We need policies that not only support the education and preparation of our workforce (so that our people have the baseline competencies necessary for the jobs of the future), but also encourage organizations to bridge the gap between education and the working world.

With the federal Race to the Top investment fund, Education Secretary Arne Duncan commands more resources dedicated to systematic education reform than all of his predecessors combined—but it still represents less than 1 percent of the roughly $650 billion we spend on K-12 education in the U.S. each year.[89] The Health Care and Education Reconciliation Act of 2010 marked tremendous progress. The legislation includes investments to increase Pell Grants by $36 billion, invest $4 billion in our nation's community college system and schools supporting minorities, cap student loan payment requirements at 10 percent of a graduate's income, and offer graduates entering public service—including teaching—complete loan forgiveness after 10 years.[90] But we can't stop there. Innovation is a two-part recipe, and education reform alone will not solve it.

Financial incentives for employers to encourage their investment in young talent might help. One type of incentive could be financial—in the form of tax credits. In Singapore, the government has created a "Productivity and Innovation" tax credit to encourage companies to invest in R&D, intellectual property development, design, and training of employees. Effective in the 2010 budget, companies get reimbursed 250 percent of their expenditures in these areas—clearly demonstrating that innovation is an important national priority.[91]

Perhaps we can provide tax credits to companies whose employees allocate a portion of their time to teaching. We could create tax-advantaged "teaching sabbaticals," for instance, that bring in qualified, motivated instructors from the private sector to serve as teachers' aides for a semester of middle-school math or high-school chemistry. Subsidies of that nature could even help employers reduce layoffs, keeping more people employed. And companies (of, perhaps, 100 employees or larger) who choose not to or are unable to participate could be required to pay a small levy, much in the same manner we fund unemployment benefits.

Or we could take it up a notch. What about requiring people to volunteer at schools as part of their eligibility for Social Security benefits? Rather than a military draft, why not create an "education draft" where qualified people are enlisted in an education rotation to teach the next generation and share their insights and knowledge in a uniform, systematic way? We can also structure tax incentives that benefit both employers and employees who take structured "classroom sabbaticals" as teachers and professors. Or we can tie government contracts and grants to education by requiring reciprocal education rotations of workers from companies receiving those grants.

The key point is that education reform on its own can't fix the problem—the government must step in, and the private sector must step up. Teachers can't prepare our next generation workforce on their own—innovation requires a connection between the new thinkers and the people working on the front lines of our economy, and we must build a bridge.

The good news is that a considerable amount of pro-innovation legislation is currently under consideration by the federal government—from investments in R&D to funding scholarships to expanding access to broadband. These are all great ideas, and the focus on innovation is pointed in the right direction. We must have innovation-friendly policy to compete.

But we don't need to wait for Washington…

The Time to Act is Now

The government must set the conditions and policies that support innovation, and the leaders among us who have the power to influence thousands or millions of people bear a special responsibility to use that power to make a difference on a large scale.

But *every one of us* can make a difference. We don't need to wait for Washington to create sweeping policies and laws—we can, and must, start now. Here are some simple steps we can take to get started.

➤ *Give Students Experience*

As Austan Goolsbee, a member of Obama's Council on Economic Advisors, explains, "Graduates' first jobs have an inordinate impact on their career path and [lifetime earnings]."[92] Experience is an essential part of preparing for success. One component of giving people "experience" is education, but experience is much broader than what happens in the classroom. Experience also includes the very important hands-on, practical perspective that comes from learning by doing. Experience includes the exposure to people who serve as coaches, role models, and boosters. Experience includes the exposure to problems—and problem solving—that is required to fuel new ideas and new thinking—the key ingredients of innovation. This isn't done in a classroom—in fact, it can't be done in a classroom. It can *only* come from experience. The way to prepare people to innovate is to give them education *and* experience.

One idea that can be implemented very quickly by every professional in the working world: reserve some roles in your organization for students while they are still in school. Train the next-generation workforce *while also* creating value for your organization and employees. You'll find that students have genuine value to contribute to the organization, even as they continue to learn. Hire students for near-term projects, internships, and job-shadows. It's one of the most cost-effective ways to bring students into the working world—and for our country's economy to benefit from their help.

If you don't have an internship program, or aren't "authorized" to bring on interns, my first piece of advice is to immediately fire your HR team—on the grounds that they are setting your organization up to fail. Beyond that, here's an alternative way to get the *Gen Y Way* into your organization: student projects. Create project-based assignments that students can work on (on-site or from their campuses). By exposing students to projects (such as competitive or market research), they benefit from learning what you're trying to accomplish—and you benefit from seeing how their new thinking brings a new perspective to the assignment. Trust me, you will learn just as much as they will.

Another option? Spend time with students by volunteering. Connect with local teachers and offer to contribute to a class or help with a project—or invite students to join your team to volunteer on a group effort, like doing a build with Habitat for Humanity. Working together to support organizations like Junior Achievement, Teach for America, AmeriCorps, The Peace Corps, Habitat for Humanity, and other similar groups creates benefits in every direction—not the least of which is bringing together new thinkers with our professionals on the front lines. It's time to stop ignoring the evidence—fusion really works.

➤ Role Models & Mentors

Although there is extensive focus on the dwindling numbers of STEM students coming out of our education system, Hal Salzman from Rutgers University suggests that the problem isn't that kids are avoiding STEM-related classes, it's that they aren't pursuing careers in their fields of study.[93] And, as Christina Romer, chairman of Obama's Council of Economic Advisors, notes, "Some of our brightest minds make small fortunes arranging the deals, rather than pursuing potentially more socially valuable careers in such fields as science, medicine, and education." Perhaps the recent financial collapse has a silver lining: the *Harvard Crimson* reported that the percentage of 2009 graduates entering finance or consulting was 20 percent, significantly lower than the 47 percent pursuing that path in 2007.[94]

If we want to encourage our students—especially those with an interest in and aptitude for analytical thinking—to pursue careers that lead to innovation, we should take every step possible to inspire them.

Furthermore, role models have the power to inspire more students to stay in school. The lack of inspiration and encouragement is the biggest factor leading to students dropping out of high school or college. A study by the Gates Foundation found that high school dropouts had a C average—they weren't failing, they were choosing to leave.[95] Without social support, role models, or encouragement, it's hard for students to see themselves following a path into the future. They believe education is not for them or they simply can't see the point. I'd like to suggest that students don't appreciate the true value of education as *a direct result* of the fact that the private sector is too far removed from the education system. Even students paying six-figure sums for college degrees aren't finding the connection with employers. And that gap creates strong doubts.

We have the power to turn this around.

Many large organizations have formal mentoring programs in which senior employees are assigned to new hires and are responsible for helping guide them as they transition into the working world and launch their careers. These programs take on an entirely new meaning today, because "reverse mentoring" happens as well. Millennials train the higher-ups on the latest technologies, social networking, and trends. Exposure to the new thinking of the *Gen Y Way* gives the mentors the chance to learn, too.

I recommend organizations take mentoring a step further, and adopt a broader view. Why not extend the concept beyond your company's walls? Encouraging your people to engage with students while they are still in high school or college goes even further to help support the up-and-coming workforce. Companies that have taken steps in this direction have found that they can create a pipeline of talent *while also* increasing the retention and commitment of star employees—because employees want to work for companies that are committed to the future. Millennials, in particular, thrive on these collaborations that create a culture of connection rather than distance.

And then let's expand it globally—there's no reason such an approach can't scale up. With today's technology, there's no reason our efforts must stop at our borders. There are Millennials all around the world who have something to teach us, if we're ready to learn.

These simple steps don't require grandiose plans or programs. If every American in our workforce committed to connecting with just *one* student a year, each and every student would have multiple mentors to learn from and we would have access to the new thinking—and new thinkers—who can, and will, shape the future of this country. As we seek to close the academic-industry gap, it's important to remember this simple truth: we are *all* teachers. And we are all students, too.

Game On ...

These steps aren't hard—they just need to happen. As one of my favorite American-made slogans says, it's time to "Just Do It."

Bridging the gap between education and the working world is more than a pragmatic choice—it's an imperative. Preparing the next generation for success is not the sole responsibility of the education system, and if we rely solely on traditional teachers to do all of the teaching, the academia-industry gap will not shrink. In fact, it will grow. All of us are teachers who can model, instruct, guide, and mentor. And we all own this problem. Let's stop debating over the class sizes our teachers must manage, and *step in to help them.* Imagine—instead of one teacher for 25 students we could have 25 teachers for each student....

Think about what a tremendous improvement it will be when more of our students graduate and emerge from college knowing far more about workplace culture, expectations, industry jargon, and the pragmatics of a multi-decade career. Think of how powerful our workforce will be when every citizen is prepared for leadership, communication, problem-solving and innovation. And think about how successful our companies and economy will be when armed with the new thinking of the Gen Y Way.

CHAPTER 8

The Way Forward

"To grow an oak tree, the best day to plant the seed was thirty years ago. The second best day is today."

Proverb

Americans have a long legacy of innovation. From telephones and televisions to light bulbs and life-saving vaccines, the innovations we've created have led to growth and prosperity around the globe.

The reason we're so innovative? Perhaps the cliché is true: it's out of necessity. Certainly, we need healthcare, smarter pollution-control technologies, and faster computers. But perhaps there is an even more fundamental reason for our multi-decade history of innovation. Perhaps we've been innovative because we have attracted and developed people who are prepared to *be* innovative—and we've created the conditions to help innovators succeed.

Our president has called us out: "The time has come for America to lead again." We must stop staying stuck in the old ways of doing things, holding on to old thinking, old expectations, old traditions, and old methods that simply do not work. We need a new perspective that is global in scope, iterative in nature, fast-paced, action-oriented—and, most importantly, committed to replacing talk with action. The good news is that the instincts that come naturally to Gen Y are exactly what we need to pull our country out of this downward spiral. Let's not stand in their way.

It's time to use our secret weapon—our new thinkers and their *Gen Y Way* that can bring the new perspective we so desperately need. Working together, we can re-start our innovation engine—and use new thinking to accelerate and focus the recovery of financial systems, schools, the government, health care, the environment, and more. Our fastest way out of these challenges is to help this next generation contribute faster. Engaging the help of our Gen Y talent is not about "paying it forward," it's not about long-term investments that will pay off sometime in the future, and it's not about altruism—we *need* their new thinking, and we need it *now*. New thinking is required for innovation, and innovation is the *only* way forward to broad and lasting prosperity.

The problems we're addressing can seem so large, so intractable, and so persistent that they almost feel impossible to untangle. At first glance, the issues of education and the workforce might appear to be too daunting, too huge to take on. It's tempting to say, "Not my problem" or "It's too long-term for me to worry about" or "It's too late to make a difference." But let me be crystal-clear here: this is <u>our</u> problem. *Our* future depends on solving this problem. *Your* job, your income, your healthcare, your ability to preserve or improve your standard of living, your ability to send your children to school and live in a safe neighborhood—these are all at risk if we don't fix things.

We *know* the problems are urgent, but, in some ways, our paralysis is rooted in the sheer scope and scale of the challenge. For whatever reason, we are acting as though this is "someone else's" problem—that "someone else" will fix it.

It's like a large-scale bystander effect. In the 1960s, Kitty Genovese[96] was murdered in New York City. Her piercing screams were heard by dozens of neighbors through adjacent walls or alleyway windows, yet no one called the police. Subsequent interviews with these bystanders revealed that they assumed someone else would take responsibility—that, surely, someone else had called the police. But no one did.

I prefer, instead, to think of a different bystander, Lenny Skutnik. In January 1982, Air Florida Flight 90 plunged into the icy Potomac River.[97] As hundreds of bystanders—including dozens of public-safety professionals—watched, rescuers repeatedly lowered a line from helicopters to one injured woman who was too weak to grasp the line. Unable to watch any longer, Skutnik—in a fierce snowstorm—ripped off his coat and boots, dove into the freezing water, swam out to the woman and pulled her to shore, saving her life. It was a stirring example of heroism, and the whole country watched it unfold. On a larger scale, we all need to be Lenny Skutniks. Let's resolve to stop watching from the shore, waiting for someone else to be the hero. Let's dive in and start fixing this problem. Let's take a page from the Millennials' playbook, and stop thinking—and start doing. The way forward is the way through.

We are at a turning point, and it's time to reaffirm what it is that has always made America so special—and so successful. At our core, we are not a nation of wallets and weapons—we are a people of ideas and ideals. Yes, we're facing serious challenges – that are of our own making and will require new thinking. We *will* emerge from today's challenges as a more prosperous, more peaceful, more vibrant nation. And the solution can be—as it always has been, and always will be—found within our people ...

People *Are* Our Most Important Asset

No one person made America great. Our country and our values have been shaped by many Americans—by the inclusion of many voices, many viewpoints, and many votes. But that doesn't mean we must leave the task to "the many."

On Dec. 1, 1955, Rosa Parks didn't envision a Montgomery Bus Boycott or a civil rights movement as she rode the bus. But she proved that one person can make a world-changing difference *because the small action inspires others to take action, too.*

Millennials have seen ample evidence that small actions are valuable—less for their inherent impact than for their ability to inspire others. It's the exponential power of the example that matters most. Small steps we take as individuals can be the spark of a wildfire, not just a drop in the ocean.

Remember the fable about the jar with the big rock, pebbles, and the sand. The challenge is to fill the jar with all of the material. If you start with the sand and pebbles first, when it's time to fit the big rock inside, there won't be enough room. But if you put the big rock in *first*, then add the pebbles, and then the sand, everything fits in the jar.

It's the same story for our society. But the biggest rock isn't simply "education" (or healthcare or energy or any other issue). It's our *people*—and our collective ability to innovate. All of the other issues—crime rates, substance abuse, environmental concerns, healthcare—they are the pebbles and sand. If we prepare our people to solve new problems in new ways—again, and again, and again—then we'll be prepared to tackle the other problems, too.

There may be some people that think the suggestions in this book are too socialist in nature—and that, in a competitive world, there are winners and losers, and that's OK. This cynical view is usually found among the highly educated 'haves' in our society, the ones who feel that the system has worked for them, so it's not that broken. In fact, it's not unusual for these people to feel a need to *protect* the current system in order to make sure that their children can continue to enjoy an advantage. They're the 'haves' who can afford all the best schools, and are connected enough to get their kids onto the right path with enrollment into the best colleges, access to the best mentors, and placement into valuable internships through their personal connections. They rationalize that if they're able to work the system to their advantage, why change it?

That logic makes sense … right up until it doesn't. Eventually, there is a tipping point—and when the weight of the 'have-nots' becomes too heavy for the 'haves' to shoulder, the society crumbles, taking the 'haves' down with it.

To me, one of the most ominous findings of the math and science skills benchmarking study was that the U.S. was the *only* country that had relatively high percentages of students in *both* the highest-performing and lowest-performing categories.[98] The gap between the haves and the have-nots is growing—and that gap may turn out to be the Achilles heel that topples the world's most powerful nation.

But maybe there's another way forward.

Maybe Americans will heed the warning signs, and sound the alarm. Maybe the crisis our nation is suffering will spark a revolution among our people who see that a new approach is needed, and inspire them to insist on changing our course. And it wouldn't be the first time Americans revolted against old thinking. In fact, that's how America became America in the first place.

Some skeptics convey a sense of arrogance—as if America is too strong to fail. We have such a significant edge over the rest of the world, and so many fundamental advantages. What we're suffering today, they reason, is just a rough patch; they believe this cycle will turn itself around, just as all other down economies have done in the past.

That sentiment is probably similar to how the elites in England viewed the "rebels across the pond." After all, the rebels didn't even have a formal military to speak of, while the royal military was the world's most powerful and highly trained. The only problem was that they were trained in old thinking that no longer worked. The rebels had a different kind of power—they had the power of a new perspective. The rebels saw a different way forward. They saw new possibilities. They had the courage to use new thinking to solve new problems in new ways. They were innovators. And you know how the story played out—the innovators won.

In fact, the innovators *always* win.

Recommended
Gen Y Books and Blogs

Jenny Floren: www.theinnovationgeneration.com and www.thegenyway.com

Experience: http://blog.experience.com

Dan Schawbel: www.personalbrandingblog.com

Penelope Trunk: http://blog.penelopetrunk.com

Lindsey Pollak: www.gettingfromcollegetocareer.com

Anya Kamenetz: http://anyakamenetz.blogspot.com/

Matt Cheuvront: www.lifewithoutpants.com

Phil Gardner: http://www.ceri.msu.edu/

Sheila Curran and Suzanne Greenwald: *Smart Moves for Liberal Arts Grads: Finding a Path to Your Perfect Career.* Ten Speed Press, 2006.

Don Tapscott: *Grown Up Digital: How the Net Generation is Changing Your World.* McGraw Hill, 2009.

Lindsey Pollak: *Getting From College to Career.* Collins, 2007.

John Zogby: *The Way We'll Be.* Random House, 2008.

Bruce Tulgan: *Not Everyone Gets a Trophy: How to Manage Generation Y.* Jossey-Bass, 2009.

Neil Howe and William Strauss: *Millennials Rising.* Vintage Books, 2000.

Laurence Kotlikoff and Scott Burns: *The Coming Generational Storm: What You Need to Know About America's Economic Future.* MIT Press, 2004.

Roger Herman, Tom Olivo, and Joyce Gioia: *Impending Crisis: Too Many Jobs, Too Few People.* Oakhill Press, 2003.

Lisa Orrell: *Millennials Incorporated.* Intelligent Women Publishing, 2007.

Judy Estrin: *Closing the Innovation Gap.* McGraw Hill, 2009.

Bea Fields, Scott Wilder, Jim Bunch & Rob Newbold: *Millennial Leaders.* Writers of the Round Table Press, 2008.

Endnotes

Chapter 1

1   Richtel, Matt. "Tech Recruiting Clashes with Immigration Rules," *The New York Times*, April 11, 2009.

2   Peter G. Peterson Foundation. "State of the Union's Finances: A Citizen's Guide," March 2009. http://www.pgpf.org/resources/PGPF_CitizensGuide_2009.pdf

3   Ip, Greg. "Time to Rebalance," *The Economist*. April 3-9, 2010.

4   Rowley, Ian and Hall, Kenji. "Japan's Lost Generation," *Business Week*, May 17, 2007.

Chapter 2

5   Cole, August & Sanders, Peter. "Air Force Resumes Tanker Contest." *The Wall Street Journal*, Sept. 25, 2009.

6   Doerr, John & Immelt, Jeff. "Falling Behind On Green Tech," *The Washington Post*, Aug. 3, 2009.

7   Ezell, Stephen. "America and the World: We're Number 40!" The International Technology & Innovation Foundation, September 2009. www.itif.org

8   Atkinson, Robert and Andes, Scott. "The Atlantic Century: Benchmarking EU and US Innovation and Competitiveness," ITIF, February 2009. www.itif.org

9   Bhide, Amar. "Debates: Innovation/Statements." www.economist.com

10 Peck, Don. "How a new jobless era will transform America," *The Atlantic*, March 2010.

11 Kristof, Nicholas. "Escaping from Poverty," *The New York Times*. March 25, 2010.

12 Westly, Erica. "150th Anniversary of the Pony Express," *Fast Company*. No. 144, April 2010.

13 Linden, Greg, Dedrick, Jason & Kraemer Kenneth L.. "Innovation and Job Creation in a Global Economy: The Case of Apple's iPod," Personal Computing Industry Center, UC Irvine, January 2009. http://pcic.merage.uci.edu

14 Kiviat, Barbara. "Jobs: where they are and how to find them", *Time*. March 29, 2010.

15 Porter, Michael, Ketels, Christian & Delgado, Mercedes . "The Microeconomic Foundations of Prosperity," *Quarterly Journal of Economics*, 2007. http://ideas.repec.org

16 Hanushek, Eric et al. "The High Cost of Low Educational Performance," Programme for International Student Assessment and OECD, 2010. http://edpro.stanford.edu/hanushek

17 Autor, David, Levy, Frank & Murnane, Richard, "The Skill Content of Recent Technological Change," MIT Press, 2003.

18 Barlow, Ed. www.creatingthefuture.com

19 Kurzweil, Ray. www.KurzweilAI.net

20 Partnership for 21st Century Skills: www.21stcenturyskills.org

21 Senge, Peter, *The Fifth Discipline*. Doubleday Business, 1994.

22 National Center on Education and the Economy. "Tough Choices or Tough Times, the New Commission on the Skills of the American Workforce," 2007. www.skillscommission.org

23 Friedman, Thomas L. "Invent, Invent, Invent," *The New York Times*, June 28, 2009.

Chapter 3

24 "Leading Tech CEOs Bring Clear Message to Washington: Innovation Critical to Creating Jobs, Growing U.S. Economy," March 23, 2010. www.technet.org Zogby International survey commissioned by Technet.

25 Murray, Alan. "Why We're Failing Math and Science," *The Wall Street Journal*, Oct. 26, 2009.

26 National Center for Education Statistics, "High School Dropout and Completion Rates in the United States: 2007." http://nces.ed.gov

27 Hauptman, Arthur M. and Kim, Young. "Cost, Commitment, and Attainment in Higher Education: An International Comparison," Jobs for the Future, May 2009. www.jff.org

[28] Hussar, William J. & Bailey, Tabitha M. "Projections of Educational Statistics to 2018: Thirty-seventh edition," National Center for Education Statistics, 2009. http://nces.ed.gov
U.S. Census Bureau. "Population Projections of the United States by Age, Sex, Race and Hispanic Origin: 1995 – 2050," February 1996. www.census.gov

[29] Goldin, Claudia & Katz, Lawrence F. "The Race Between Education and Technology," Harvard University Press, 2008.

[30] Lumina Foundation: www.luminafoundation.org

[31] Bill and Melinda Gates Foundation: www.gatesfoundation.org

[32] Remarks by the President on the American Graduation Initiative: Macomb Community College, Warren MI, July 14, 2009. www.whitehouse.gov/the_press_office/

[33] Carnevale, Anthony & Derochers, Donna. "Help wanted … credentials required," Educational Testing Service, 2001.

[34] United States Bureau of Labor Statistics: www.bls.gov
"Education and Income: More Learning is Key to Higher Earnings," 2006. Occupational Outlook Quarterly, Fall 2006.

[35] Brooks, David. "The Biggest Issue," *The New York Times*, July 29, 2008.

[36] American Institute of Economic Research. "The AIER Cost of Living Guide." www.aier.org
Consumer Price Index: www.bls.gov/cpi

[37] Jan, Tracy. "Fifty thousand dollars," *The Boston Globe*, March 28, 2010.

[38] National Center for Public Policy and Higher Education. "*Measuring Up 2008*." www.highereducation.org

[39] Lewin, Tamar. "Higher Education May Soon Be Unaffordable for Most Americans," *The New York Times*, Dec. 3, 2008.

[40] Wellman, Jane. "Trends in College Spending," Delta Project, 2009. Delta Cost Project: www.deltacostproject.org

[41] State Higher Education Executive Officers, "State Higher Education Finance FY 2008." www.sheeo.org

[42] College Board: www.collegeboard.org
http://connection-collegeboard.com (summary of education statistics)

43 Baum, Sandy et al. "Trends in Student Aid," College Board, 2009. www.collegeboard.com/trends

44 United States Department of Education – Official Cohort Default Rates for Schools http://www2.ed.gov/offices/OSFAP/defaultmanagement/cdr.html

45 Kamenetz, Anya. *DIY U: Edupunks, Edupreneurs, and the Coming Transformation of Higher Education*. Chelsea Green Publishing Company: White River Jct., VT. 2010.

Chapter 4

46 National Assessment of Educational Progress ("Nation's Report Card"): http://nces.ed.gov/nationsreportcard/

47 Rotella, Carlo. "Class Warrior," *The New Yorker*. Feb. 1, 2010.

48 Martin, Dr. Michael & Mullis, Dr. Ina et al. "Trends in International Mathematics and Science Study (TIMSS)," 1995-2007. www.iea.nl

49 Organization for Economic Development and Cooperation, "2006 Programme for Student Assessment (PISA)," 2007. www.oecd.org

50 Ingersoll, Richard M. "Teaching Science in the 21st Century," National Science Teachers Association, April 30, 2007. www.nsta.org

51 McCartney, Kathleen. "Letter to the Editor," *The New York Times*. March 25, 2010.

52 Conference Board: www.conference-board.org "New Report Shows Employers Struggle with Ill-Prepared Workforce," July 14, 2009.

53 Coy, Peter. "Help Wanted," *Business Week*, May 22, 2009.

54 ITT Educational Services, Inc. Financial results as presented during the earnings conference call on Jan. 21, 2010. www.ittesi.com

55 Andreasson, Kim et al. "Global Education 20/20," The Economist Intelligence Unit, March 2009.

56 Rosenberg, Debra. "What's college for, anyway?" *Newsweek*, Oct. 26, 2009.

57 Kamenetz, Anya. *DIY U: Edupunks, Edupreneurs, and the Coming Transformation of Higher Education*. Chelsea Green Publishing Company: White River Jct., VT. 2010.

[58] Bernard, Tara Siegel. "Math, Civics, and How to Budget." *The New York Times*, April 10, 2010, page B1.

[59] Council for Economic Education: "Report Card – Survey of the States" and "Teachers Use Technology, Competitions to Teach Basic Personal Finance Skills." www.councilforeconed.org

[60] Kamenetz, Anya. "A is for App," *Fast Company*. No. 144, April 2010.

[61] Thomas, Evan and Wingert, Pat. "F: Why we can't get rid of failing teachers." *Newsweek*, March 15, 2010, page 24.

[62] Brill, Steven. "The Rubber Room." *The New Yorker*, Aug. 31, 2009.

Chapter 5

[63] Zogby, John. The Way We'll Be. Random House: New York, NY. 2008.

Chapter 6

[64] Lohr, Steve. "Inventor Whose Pioneer PC Helped Inspire Microsoft Dies," *The New York Times*, April 3, 2010.

[65] Infinite Energy: The Magazine of New Energy Science & Technology: http://www.infinite-energy.com/

[66] Coy, Peter. "Help Wanted," *Business Week*, May 22, 2009.

[67] Conference Board: "The Ill-prepared U.S. Workforce: Exploring the Challenges of Employer-Provided Workforce Solutions," July 2009. www.conference-board.org

[68] Krugman, Paul. "Green Economics: How we can afford to tackle climate change." *The New York Times Magazine*, April 11, 2010.

[69] United States Bureau of Labor Statistics: www.bls.gov

[70] Experience.com research can be found at http://blog.experience.com

[71] NASA: http://www.nasa.gov/centers/kennedy
Presentation by Dr. Gregg Buckingham at the Future Workforce Solutions Conference, March 2008.

[72] Zain: 2008 Annual Report. www.zain.com
Interview with Dina Saad, 2009.
F.U.N.: http://www.ameinfo.com/212544.html

[73] McGirt, Ellen. "How Chris Hughes Helped Launch Facebook and the Barack Obama Campaign," *Fast Company*, April 1, 2009.

Chapter 7

[74] Microsoft Students to Business: http://s2b.experience.com
Microsoft, Windows, Exchange and XBOX are trademarks of Microsoft Corporation.

[75] Intel Science Talent Search: http://www.societyforscience.org/STS

[76] Friedman, Thomas L. "America's Real Dream Team," *The New York Times*, March 21, 2010.

[77] Bucknell University Career Development Center and Externship Program: http://www.bucknell.edu/x2688.xml

[78] Governor's School, South Carolina: Summer Program for Research Interns http://www.scgssm.org/prospective_students/outreach_programs/spri/

[79] Rockefeller Center at Dartmouth College: http://rockefeller.dartmouth.edu/

[80] Duke University: http://www.studentaffairs.duke.edu/career

[81] Sheila Curran: http://curranoncareers.com/

[82] Vanderkam, Laura. "Get a job? No, make a job," USA Today. Feb. 6, 2007.

[83] Kristof, Nicholas D. "Escaping from Poverty," The New York Times, March 25, 2010.

[84] Austin Kiviat, Barbara. "Jobs: Where they are and how to find them." *Time*, March 29, 2010.
Bootstrap Austin: http://www.bootstrapaustin.org/
Austin Technology Incubator: http://www.ati.utexas.edu/
Workforce Solutions: http://www.wfscapitalarea.com/
Thomas, Scott G. "Young in the city," Portfolio.com, March 15, 2010.

[85] Scott Kirsner. "Youth Movement." *The Innovation Economy*, February 17, 2008. http://www.boston.com/business/technology/innoeco/

[86] FIRST Robotics: http://www.usfirst.org/

87 Lockheed-Martin http://www.lockheedmartin.com/aboutus/community/education/index.html

88 Ezell, Stephen. "America and the World: We're 40!" *Democracy Journal*, Fall 2009. www.democracyjournal.org and www.itif.org

89 Rotella, Carlo. "Class Warrior," *The New Yorker*, Feb. 1, 2010.

90 United States Department of Education: Race to the Top Fund: http://www2.ed.gov/programs/racetothetop/index.html Health Care and Education Reconciliation Act of 2010: http://www.whitehouse.gov/blog/2010/04/15/giving-back-students

91 Inland Revenue Authority of Singapore: Productivity and Innovation Credit: http://www.iras.gov.sg/irashome/PIcredit.aspx

92 Peck, Don. "How a new jobless era will transform America," *The Atlantic*, March 2010.

93 Salzman, Hal, Lowell, Lindsey, Bernstein, Hamutal & Henderson, Everett. "Steady as She Goes? Three Generations of Students through the Science and Engineering Pipeline." Paper presented at Annual Meetings of the Association for Public Policy Analysis and Management Washington, D.C. Nov. 5-7, 2009. http://policy.rutgers.edu/faculty/salzman/

94 Kountz, Candice. "The Siren Call," *Harvard Political Review*, Dec. 20, 2009.

95 Atkinson, Robert. "Eight Ideas for Improving the America COMPETES Act," ITIF, March 2010. www.itif.org

Chapter 8

96 Kitty Genovese and the "Bystander Effect": http://en.wikipedia.org/wiki/Bystander_effect

97 Montes, Sue Anne Pressley. "In a Moment of Horror, Rousing Acts of Courage," *The Washington Post*, Jan. 13, 2007. The story of Lenny Skutnik.

98 The Conference Board: "Facts for Education Advocates—International Comparisons," 2004.

About the Author

In *The Innovation Generation*, Jenny Floren explains why the emerging talent of *Millennials* is so special, and why their new thinking—the *Gen Y Way*—is so important to America's success in the global economy.

From her own experience as an entrepreneur, she knows firsthand what it means to challenge old thinking in the pursuit of innovation. Inspired by her younger sister's quest for the right post-college job, Jenny hopped off the corporate ladder and launched Experience.com in 1996—and she hasn't looked back since.

For over a decade, Jenny's groundbreaking vision for how to enlist educational institutions, companies, governments and citizens around the world to educate, assist and inspire the next generation of talent has been recognized by national press and industry leaders throughout academia and enterprise. Millions of students and over 100,000 employers have directly benefited from Jenny's innovative way of bridging the gap between college and the working world—so both sides of the table find the best fit, and accelerate success.

Jenny is a frequent speaker at nationwide universities and major business events to share her unique perspective on the up-and-coming workforce. She earned a BA in psychology from Dartmouth College and was a management consultant with Bain & Company in Boston prior to starting Experience. She also serves on the Board of Directors of Jobs for the Future, the Rockefeller Center for Public Policy, and the Massachusetts Innovation & Technology Exchange.

To contact Jenny ...

Twitter: twitter.com/JennyFloren

LinkedIn: linkedin.com/in/jfloren

Facebook: facebook.com/jfloren

Email: jf@experience.com

Blog: blog.experience.com

Breinigsville, PA USA
19 September 2010
245651BV00005B/1/P